Your Guide to VA Loans

How to Cut Through the Red Tape and Get Your Dream Home Fast

David Reed

⫶AMACOM

American Management Association

New York • Atlanta • Brussels • Chicago • Mexico City • San Francisco
Shanghai • Tokyo • Toronto • Washington, D.C.

Special discounts on bulk quantities of AMACOM books are
available to corporations, professional associations, and other
organizations. For details, contact Special Sales Department,
AMACOM, a division of American Management Association,
1601 Broadway, New York, NY 10019.
Tel.: 212–903–8316. Fax: 212–903–8083.
E-mail: specialsls@amanet.org
Website: www.amacombooks.org/go/specialsales
To view all AMACOM titles go to: www.amacombooks.org

This publication is designed to provide accurate and authoritative
information in regard to the subject matter covered. It is sold with the
understanding that the publisher is not engaged in rendering legal,
accounting, or other professional service. If legal advice or other expert
assistance is required, the services of a competent professional person
should be sought.

Library of Congress Cataloging-in-Publication Data
    Reed, David, 1957 Oct. 1-
        Your guide to VA loans : how to cut through the red tape and get your
    dream home fast / David Reed.
            p.   cm.
        Includes index. 7927861
        ISBN-13: 978–0-8144–7435–8
        ISBN-10: 0-8144–7435–7
            1. Mortgage loans—United States.   2. Veterans—Loans—United States.
    3. Mortgage guarantee insurance—United States.   4. House buying—United
    States.   5. United States. Veterans Administration.   I. Title.
        HG2040.5.U5R4328   2008
        332.7'22—dc22   2007021983

Printed in the United States of America.

Printing number

10   9   8   7   6   5   4   3   2   1

To the men and women who serve and protect our country. And especially to an uncle I never met . . . because he died 12 years before I was even born.

PFc Leroy Cartmill was with the 507th Parachute Infantry Regiment of the 17th Airborne Division. He was a paratrooper. On March 24, 1945, PFc Leroy Cartmill was KIA during an offensive near Wesel, Germany, and is buried in an American military cemetery in Margraten, Holland.

He served with his two brothers, Uncle Dale and Uncle Earl, who are still living in Oklahoma, and whom I respect so very much. I never met Uncle Leroy, but I am proud of him.

God Bless Uncle Leroy. And God Bless America.

Contents

Introduction

Homeownership levels in the United States have reached record highs. It seems everyone is buying a home. In fact, nearly 70 percent of all Americans are homeowners. Do you want to be included in that number? If you do, answer a few questions.

Before you dive headfirst into filling out all the required mortgage forms and determining eligibility status, you need to ask yourself if you're really ready to buy. If you're a first-time homebuyer, this is a critical question.

Are you buying now because you want to, or are you buying because everyone tells you that you *should* own your own home? Owning a home is perhaps one of the quickest ways to establish a positive net worth. As your home increases in value, so does your net worth. As you pay your mortgage on time, your credit profile improves.

But when things go wrong, it's you, the homeowner, who's going to have to take care of the problems.

For example, you wake up one morning in your apartment and find out there's no hot water. What do you do? Well, you call the apartment manager and complain, that's what. Yep, all you have to do is say, "Get on over here right away and fix my hot water heater, and while you're at it, knock off a day's worth of rent for my trouble."

Or let's say you're doing some dishes and the garbage disposal goes out on you. It's filled with gunk and you don't know the first thing about garbage disposals. But wait, you're renting . . . call the landlord and pronto!

But when you own the place where you live, you own not just the home but also the hot water heater and the garbage disposal along with it. Busted hot water heater? Can you say $600? Garbage disposal? $200. Of course, you have to know how to install both or else you'll have to pay some labor charges. Plumbers are expensive. Are you financially, as well as mentally, ready to own?

One of the main benefits of Veterans Administration (VA) loans is the lack of a down payment requirement. But that doesn't mean you don't have to have money going into the deal. There are things such as closing costs and cash reserves a lender will want to verify. You'll want to have some money in the bank somewhere to take care of emergencies and general maintenance on your home.

Simply put, just because you "can" do something doesn't mean you should. You shouldn't buy a home just because someone else said you should . . . unless, of course, someone else agrees to make your mortgage payment for you.

One way to determine if you're ready to buy would be to compare what you're currently paying for rent with what a new house payment would be. Are you active duty and bunking for free? Then there's a big difference between free and paying a mortgage. But if you're paying rent and you feel comfortable with that rent payment, then start there. That monthly payment will help determine your comfort level in buying a new home and getting a mortgage.

Are you paying $2,000 in rent and it hurts each month? Are you living paycheck to paycheck with no money in the bank after writing that rent check? Then $2,000 is too much for you. Or maybe your situation is different: You pay $2,000 each month in rent but you can easily pay more—$2,500, for example, or $3,000. Without sweating, right?

Perhaps one of the first places to start would be to find an online mortgage calculator that takes into consideration your current rent payments and compares them to a mortgage payment. These calculators are everywhere online. Your bank probably has one, but the one I like best is found at www.ginniemae.gov.

It's here you'll find a Rent vs. Own calculator. It's also the place where you'll find out the Rent vs. Own calculators always tell you it's a good time to buy. More important, the website explains the benefits of having a mortgage that you can afford compared with what you pay in rent.

Rent money goes out the window. Mortgage payments go into the window. And the doors. And the roof, and so on. Mortgage payments are your equity and not your landlord's. There's a very good feeling in making a mortgage payment each month. Yeah, it's money you have to pay back. But, at the very same time, you're building equity and ownership.

A Rent vs. Own calculator will take your current rent payment and compare it to a potential mortgage payment. At the same time it will address the impact a tax-deductible mortgage payment will have on your income, as well as state and local property taxes you pay on your new home.

Didn't know that? You bet. Property taxes are a new expense when owning, but those who itemize their tax deductions on their income taxes (and most people who have a mortgage do) also get to deduct not just property taxes paid, but also the mortgage interest paid from the taxable income.

Rent vs. Own calculators examine those factors, and that's usually why such calculators always tell you that it's better to own than buy. It's not necessarily a scam by any means; it's just that the math will almost always work out to favor ownership. When the calculator doesn't favor getting a mortgage it's usually because rent payments are very low compared to current interest rates.

Now that you know you're ready and you've figured out your monthly payments, it's time to be . . . a homeowner.

CHAPTER 1

Getting Started

What is a VA loan? First and foremost, it's an entitlement. An entitlement is something that is owed to you by someone else. And you earned it. Way back in 1944, Congress enacted the GI Bill, which authorized the creation and funding of various "thank yous" to the nation's veterans in the form of health benefits, free education, and housing assistance.

What better way to thank those who served than with free health care, free education, and (almost) free housing? Back in the days before VA loans were invented, the U.S. Department of Veterans Affairs knew that its soldiers had better things to do than save up for a down payment on a house—primarily dodging bullets, defending the country, and protecting the civvies back home.

Unfortunately, VA lending hasn't been as popular as it once was, mostly due to changes at the VA itself. As the VA got bigger and bigger, things took longer and longer to get done. At the same time, other nongovernment-backed loans, such as those approved using Fannie Mae and Freddie Mac guidelines, took less and less time. A VA home loan application could take several weeks to complete. Even in the electronic era, when home loan software became available to speed up the approval process, the VA was still doing things the old-fashioned way, by hand and by mail. Loans were approved by human beings, using antiquated qualification guidelines that could quite frankly deter qualified veterans and service personnel from even applying for a VA mortgage.

Qualifying veterans began to shun the program, instead relying on conventional or government loans fashioned by the Federal National Mortgage Association (FNMA) or a HUD-guaranteed loan backed by the Federal Housing Administration (FHA). In fact, I know of Realtors who would steer people away from VA loans thinking they were nothing more than a boondoggle.

Certainly, veterans could get approved by using a VA-backed loan, yet sometimes sellers wouldn't accept a VA offer, just because it took so long to get a VA loan to closing. If a seller is entertaining two offers that are exactly the same, and one can close within two to three weeks while the VA could take six to eight weeks, which offer do you think is most likely to be accepted . . . the VA loan or the other one? That's right, the other one.

Perhaps that was true a few years ago, but nothing could be further from the truth today. The VA has become more automated, its lending guidelines and approval process altogether have become more streamlined, and VA loans can close just as quickly as any other loan type. Finally, the government caught up with itself and began implementing new technologies that were available to other loan types.

There are other loan choices available in the marketplace, and we'll address those choices in Chapter 8, but if you qualify for a VA loan and want or need a zero down loan alternative, there is no better choice in the market.

Period.

Why? Because any other zero down loan program will require a higher rate, less desirable terms, higher closing costs, and strict credit guidelines. There simply is no equivalent zero down mortgage loan in the nongovernment arena that can match a VA loan.

For instance, an interest rate for a thirty-year fixed VA loan would be almost a full percent lower than a similar zero down mortgage from a conventional lender using FNMA standards.

On a zero-money-down VA loan at 6 percent over thirty years on $200,000, the principal and interest payment works out to about $1,193 per month. For a competing zero-money-down loan using non-VA loans at 7 percent, the monthly payment goes up to $1,322, or $130 every month! That's a lot of money, and it's why you should look into a VA loan.

Sometimes VA loans are not the best choice. There are required "funding fees" that are included in all VA loans, so if you have 10 percent or more for a down payment, a VA loan may not be your best option. We'll look more closely at conventional loans as compared to VA loans in Chapter 3 to help you make that decision. For most people, though, VA loans offer a way into their dream home.

Who Qualifies for a VA Loan?

According to the Veterans Administration, there are nearly 25 million veterans alive today. There are also National Guard members, active duty personnel, and qualifying spouses of deceased veterans.

To qualify for a VA loan, you must fall into one of the following categories during wartime and during peacetime.

Wartime Service

You can qualify for a VA loan if your wartime service was during:

WWII	9/16/1940 to 7/25/1947
Korean War	6/27/1950 to 1/31/1955
Vietnam War	8/5/1964 to 5/7/1975

You must have served at least ninety days on active duty and been discharged under other than dishonorable conditions. If you served less than ninety days, you may be eligible if discharged for a service-connected disability.

Peacetime Service

Peacetime service is recognized during the periods:

7/26/1947 to 6/26/1950
2/1/1955 to 8/4/1964
5/8/1975 to 9/7/1980 (enlisted)
5/8/1975 to 10/16/1981 (officer)

You must have served at least 181 days of continuous active duty and been discharged under other than dishonorable conditions. If you served less than 181 days, you may be eligible if discharged for a service-connected disability.

Service After 9/7/1980 (Enlisted) or 10/16/1981 (Officer)

If you were separated from service that began after these dates, you must have:

- Completed twenty-four months of continuous active duty or the full period (at least 181 days) for which you were ordered or called to active duty and been discharged under conditions other than dishonorable.
- Completed at least 181 days of active duty and been discharged under the specific authority of 10 USC 1173 (Hardship) or 10 USC 1171 (Early Out) or have been determined to have a compensable service-connected disability.
- Been discharged with less than 181 days of service for a service-connected disability. Individuals may also be eligible if they were released from active duty due to an involuntary reduction in force, certain medical conditions, or, in some instances, for the convenience of the government.

Gulf War Service from 8/2/1990 to Date Yet to Be Determined

If you served on active duty during the Gulf War, you must have:

- Completed twenty-four months of continuous active duty or the full period (at least ninety days) for which you were called or ordered to active duty and been discharged under conditions other than dishonorable.
- Completed at least ninety days of active duty and been discharged under the specific authority of 10 USC 1173 (Hardship) or 10 USC 1173 (Early Out) or have been determined to have a compensable service-connected disability.

- Been discharged with less than ninety days of service for a service-connected disability. Individuals may also be eligible if they were released from active duty due to an involuntary reduction in force, certain medical conditions, or, in some instances, for the convenience of the government.

Active Duty Service Personnel

If you are now on regular duty (not active duty for training), you are eligible after having served 181 days (ninety days during the Gulf War) unless discharged or separated from a previous qualifying period of active duty service.

Selected Reserves or National Guard

If you are not otherwise eligible and you have completed a total of six years in the Selected Reserves or National Guard (as a member of an active unit who attended required weekend drills and two-week active duty for training), you are eligible for a VA loan, provided you were either:

- Discharged with an honorable discharge
- Placed on the retired list
- Transferred to the Standby Reserve or an element of the Ready Reserve other than the Selected Reserve after service characterized as honorable service, or continue to serve in the Selected Reserves

Individuals who completed less than six years may be eligible if discharged for a service-connected disability.

You may also be determined eligible if you are:

- An unremarried spouse of a veteran who died while in service or from a service-connected disability
- A spouse of a serviceperson missing in action or a prisoner of war

A surviving spouse who remarried on or after attaining age 57, and on or after December 16, 2003, may also be eligible for the home loan benefit. However, a surviving spouse who remarried *before* December 16, 2003, and on or after attaining age 57 would have had to apply no later than December 15, 2004, to establish home loan eligibility, otherwise the VA must deny applications.

Other Service

Eligibility for a VA loan may also be established for:

- Certain United States citizens who served in the armed forces of a government allied with the United States in WWII
- Individuals with service as members in certain organizations, such as Public Health Service officers; cadets at the United States Military, Air Force, or Coast Guard academies; midshipmen at the United States Naval Academy; officers of the National Oceanic and Atmospheric Administration, merchant seaman with WWII service; and others

In all cases, you must also have been honorably discharged. Dishonorable discharge would require an investigation by the VA to determine eligibility.

Step 1: Proof of Eligibility

If you fall into any of the above-mentioned categories, you next need to start completing some paperwork, beginning with obtaining your Certificate of Eligibility. This form is the legal proof to a lender that you indeed qualify for this special program. You start by filling out Form 26–1880 (Request for a Certificate of Eligibility; see Appendix C).

The form is self-explanatory, but the most important piece is Section 6, detailing your military service. This requirement is most often met by providing a copy of your DD-214 when you were discharged. If you were a member of Selected Reserves or National Guard, you need to provide a copy of your NGB Form 22, or the Report of Separation and Record of Service.

If you don't have your DD-214, you can request a copy by filling out yet one more form: Form SF-180 (see Appendix D). Complete the application and mail or fax it to the custodian nearest you. Currently, there are about fifteen custodians who keep your records.

All these forms are readily available to you by visiting www.va.gov or contacting your nearest VA center and asking them to mail, e-mail, or fax the forms to you. You can also have your lender request your Certificate of Eligibility for you simply by providing them with your DD-214 or your NGB Form 22.

Okay, I know what you're thinking: "Goodness, this doesn't sound streamlined at all." And you're right, it could be a lot more streamlined. That's why President Bush authorized the creation of the Automated Certificate of Eligibility, or ACE, in 2002.

ACE is the preferred method of obtaining your Certificate of Eligibility. Your lender requests it electronically on your behalf directly from the VA. There's one caveat, though: You'll still need to have your DD-214 or Form 22, and the ACE database may not yet be fully activated. But your lender will try ACE first. If you're not listed in ACE, the old-fashioned way will suffice.

Getting your Certificate of Eligibility directly from the VA can take up to ten days if everything is done by mail. You can also simply visit your closest VA center if you're close enough.

Even though you may not yet have your Certificate of Eligibility and have to request it, that shouldn't hold up your loan application by any means. Your lender will still process your VA loan application in anticipation of getting your certificate. We'll go into more detail on your loan application later on in this chapter, but determining your eligibility is your first step.

Request for a Certificate of Eligibility (Form 26–1880)

This form is divided into eight small sections:

1. *Your First, Middle, and Last Name.* If you got married or changed your name during service or afterward, show both last names on the form.

2. *Date of Birth.* Easy enough.

3. *Veteran's Daytime Telephone Number.* Include all numbers: work, cell, and home.

4. *Address of Veteran.* This can be your street address or a P.O. Box.

5. *Mail Certificate of Eligibility To.* Only complete this section if the certificate is to be mailed to an address other than the one you gave in Section 4.

6. *Military Service Data.* In this section you list your service dates; your name as it appears on your separation papers or Statement of Service; your Social Security number or Service Number, if it's different from your Social Security number; and finally the name of the military branch in which you served.

7. *Discharged, Retired, or Disabled Status.* This section is divided into two parts. Section 7A asks if you were discharged, retired, or separated from service due to a disability or if you now have any service-related disability. If so, then you'll have to complete Section 7B, which asks for your VA Claim File Number. Disabled veterans receive additional mortgage loan benefits, and this is the area where you document your disability status.

8. *Previous VA Loans.* Even though this form has six lines so that you can list all your previous VA loans, it specifically asks that you don't leave any lines blank but write "N/A" where applicable. Although you can only have one VA loan at a time, this section will help the VA determine any remaining benefits you may have.

It's possible that you bought a VA home, someone assumed that note, or the property is rented out. Until you sell that property or refinance into a non-VA loan, then your eligibility is tied up on that original note. Or maybe you used your VA benefit to buy a home but sold it or refinanced it to another note, releasing your VA eligibility to use again.

As a veteran, you get to use your VA home loan eligibility more than just once to buy another home as long as the previous VA loan no longer exists and you've always made your payments on time. This section of the form asks what type of property you owned, where it was located, if you still own the property, and, if not, what happened to it. It also asks for the original date on the note and the VA loan number, if you can track it down.

You can use your entitlement as many times as you want, under certain conditions. Typically if you've paid off your prior VA loan and sold the property, you can have your used eligibility restored to buy yet another home. Also, on a one-time-only basis, you may have your eligibility restored once if your prior VA loan has been paid in full but you still own the property.

That's it. Once you've filled out all eight sections of Form 26–1880, you simply sign it, mail it in, and wait.

Request Pertaining to Military Records Standard Form 180

This form is divided into three sections (see Appendix D).

Section I: Information Needed to Locate Your Records. Parts 1 through 4 ask for your basic identification information, including your name, Social Security number, and date and place of birth. Part 5 asks if you were Active, Reserve, or National Guard, then asks for your dates of service, whether you were an officer or enlisted, and finally your service number. Part 6 asks if the veteran is deceased, and Part 7 if the veteran is retired from the military.

Section II: Information and/or Documents Requested. Part 1, Report of Separation, is probably the most common request for getting your DD-214. There are two boxes to check as well: Undeleted or Deleted.

An Undeleted report is simply a copy of all the information regarding your separation. If you want the DD-214, it's the Undeleted report you want. Everything about your discharge will be in this file. A Deleted report is similar to the Undeleted one, but it leaves out information regarding authority for separation, reason for separation, re-enlistment eligibility code, and character of separation.

Part 2 asks for any other documentation or forms you need other than the DD-214. Part 3 asks you why you want the information.

Section III: Return Address and Signature. This is where you execute the request by signing and dating the request and indicating who you are. There is a separate page on the SF-180 that lists the addresses where you're supposed to send your request, depending on where and when you served.

Maximum Loan Amounts

The VA recently made a significant change to VA loan guaranty amounts. Before the change, those amounts were sometimes so low that they were unattractive. Let's say the veteran wanted to buy a $400,000 home but the VA guaranty was $60,000. Four times the guaranty means the maximum loan amount for a VA lender is $240,000. In this case, because the VA loan limit is lower than conventional loans, the veteran would be better off going for a conventional loan. These guaranty amounts have gradually increased over the years using a VA guaranty formula, but to be more competitive with the conventional market, VA guaranty amounts are now pegged to conventional loan limits. If the conventional loan limit is $417,000, then the VA will guarantee one-fourth of that amount, or $104,250.

Loan limits don't have to change every year, but they usually do. Each year, in October, the national median housing price is calculated. If there is a 10 percent increase in home prices year over year, the conventional and VA loan limits will also increase by 10 percent for that year. No change in home prices? No change in loan limits.

Because of this change, VA loans are now on par with other conventional or nongovernment home loans with regard to loan size. Because they also offer lower mortgage rates when compared to other zero down loans, VA loans are usually the hands-down choice for eligible borrowers.

Step 2: Preapproval from the Lender

Getting preapproved means you complete a loan application with a lender who reviews your income, your credit, and your assets. The lender then provides you with a piece of paper that says you're ready to go shopping because you've already been approved by your lender.

Your story begins with your loan application. The mortgage application is a five-page form that is divided into ten sections. One thing you'll notice is that there is no such thing as a "VA" loan application. Instead, one loan application covers all residential loans, including VA loans, and it's named after the Fannie Mae Form 1003—appropriately called "the ten-oh-three."

These ten sections are appropriated as:

1. Type of Mortgage and Loan Terms

2. Property Information and Purpose of Loan

3. Borrower Information

4. Employment Information

5. Monthly Income and Housing Expense Information

6. Assets and Liabilities

7. Details of Transaction

8. Declarations

9. Acknowledgment and Agreement

10. Information for Government Monitoring Purposes

And you thought the military had a corner on forms.

At last count, there were about 350 boxes to be completed on the 1003. Yes, it can be intimidating and, yes, the mortgage business has secret code words just like you're used to, but taking them one section at a time makes it a little easier to swallow. We'll do that here.

Section 1: Type of Mortgage and Loan Terms

The very first thing your 1003 asks you is what type of mortgage you're applying for: conventional, FHA, VA, or other. Many consumers won't know which type they need or if they're eligible for one or more of these loan types. You're VA eligible, so choose VA. You can change your mind later if you want, but for now, check this box.

This section also has a place for you to choose a fixed rate, an adjustable rate, the term of the loan (how many months or years), the requested loan amount, and, of course, "other." This part of the 1003, like the other sections, can be changed throughout the application process, so if you check that you want a fixed rate and change your mind later, you won't need to complete an entire new application. Just make the changes needed.

VA loan offerings can have fixed or adjustable interest rates, depending upon when or if Congress allows for them. VA loans always come in the fixed variety, and sometimes adjustable-rate loans appear. We'll discuss loan types in more detail in Chapter 7.

Section 2: Property Information and Purpose of Loan

This is the address of the property you want to buy. You can leave it blank if you haven't found a house yet, or you can put in something like "123 Main Street" just to get an address into the system. This section will also ask you if the property is a single-family house or a multiunit property, like a duplex. A legal description of the property is also required. The borrower or lender typically doesn't have this information early on, so you'll probably leave this box blank. A legal description reads something like, "Lot II, Section A, 123 Main Subdivision." Your lender will get this information later on from the agents, from the title, or from an attorney involved in the transaction. Some Automated Underwriting System (AUS) programs require a property address to get a preapproval; in that case, use a simple "123 Main Street, Anywhere USA."

This section also asks if your request is for a refinance loan, a purchase loan, or even a construction loan. Will you live in the property or is it for a rental? Either way, you must tell if the property you're buying is going to be your primary residence, a vacation or second home, or an investment property. VA loans do not allow purchases for investment or vacation homes, so if you're applying for a VA loan, you check "primary residence."

Lenders are getting stricter about verifying whether the home being purchased is for a primary residence. Loan fraud has become a big issue over the past few years, and one of the most common tricks is checking off "primary" residence when in fact the property will be used as an investment or for a rental. Mortgage rates are higher for nonprimary properties because they carry greater risk for the lender, so they're priced accordingly. Investment properties also often require a higher down payment.

So, instead of paying more in down payment or getting a higher rate, borrowers check off "primary" residence, thinking they're saving themselves a lot of money. But the lender will find out soon enough— usually when the lender sends an employee out to the house, knocks on the door, and asks who lives there. If the lender discovers that it's not you living there, but renters, the lender will call the note in.

If you are making an application for a construction loan, there are sections that itemize the land cost and the construction cost, along with final anticipated value. For a refinance, it will ask you when you bought the property, what you paid for it, what existing liens there may be, what improvements you've made, and how much they cost.

Although the VA can guarantee construction loans, few lenders (if any) offer them because of the risks and potential disputes associated with new construction. Construction lending is a drawn-out and labor-intensive activity that doesn't fit well with keeping VA rates low. More complexity in a mortgage loan can mean higher rates. Neither you nor the VA wants that.

The final part of this section asks how you're going to hold title, be it individually or with someone else, and if you're going to own the property "fee simple" (which is outright ownership of both the land and the home) or "leasehold" (where you may own the home but the land is being leased).

How can you buy a home on someone else's land? Leaseholds can work when the lease period is for an extended period of time, say, ninety-nine years or so. This sounds odd but it is not as uncommon as you think in areas where Native American tribes may own land that has been developed with houses, shopping malls, and the like. More than likely this will never be an issue for you.

Section 3: Borrower Information

This section is about you. It gets into the "meat" of the application and identifies who you are by way of your legal name, your Social Security number, and where you live. This is the most personal part of the application because it's used to check your credit report, address, age, and phone number. Who cares how old you are? People have to reach a certain age before they can execute a sales contract. Age information can also help identify a borrower (someone who is eighteen years old shouldn't have credit lines on his or her credit report that are twenty years old, for example). Sometimes this question sounds like a loan approval question, but the fact is that it's illegal to discriminate in mortgage lending, and it's illegal to discriminate based on how old you are.

This section also asks how many years of school you've had. For the life of me, I've never understood why this question is part of a loan application, and I've never been given any good reason. It seems to be a carryover from older loan applications, where the information was used to predict future earnings. An underwriter might let the new graduate from law school borrow a little more because of the person's likely strong earnings potential.

But is a person with a GED somehow less creditworthy than someone with a Ph.D. and an MBA? Hardly. But this box is still there on the loan application; you can fill in that information if you want to, but it really doesn't matter one way or the other. It might mean something if you put in just twelve years of school but claim that you're a doctor or a dentist. Then you'll need to explain how you accomplished such a feat. Otherwise, don't worry about loans not being approved based on the number of years you've gone to school.

The final section is reserved for the number of your dependents. This box really only applies to VA mortgages that calculate household and residual income numbers, but again, it isn't something that is used to approve or deny your loan request.

If you've lived at your current address for less than two years, you'll also be asked to provide a previous address. But that's really about it. No pint of blood or firstborn offspring required. In the end, this section simply nails down exactly who you are and where you've lived.

Section 4: Employment Information

Now that we know who you are, we want to make sure you have a job, confirm how long you've been working, for whom you work, and whether you're self-employed. This section asks for your employer's name and address along with a phone number. Lenders will contact your employer—either by telephone, letter, or even e-mail (as long as the e-mail address can be verified)—asking for verification of how long you've worked there, what your job description is, and how much money you make.

You'll notice there are two separate boxes about your length of employment. One box asks for "Years on this job" and the other asks for "Years employed in this line of work or profession." Lenders look for a minimum of two years in the workforce at the same job, as a sign of job stability. They also like to see someone in the same line of work, for the very same reason. If you've not been at your current job for two years, don't worry, as long as you've done the same or similar line of work somewhere else.

Have you been laid off because of an economic downturn? Document the dates and reasons for the time not worked. If you've been a store manager at your current job for six months, all you need to do is document your previous jobs for at least another eighteen months to make up your two-year minimum. There's another box for listing previous employers, asking for the same contact information along with how much money you made at your old jobs. Finally, you'll be asked about your job title, the type of business you're in, and whether you're self-employed.

If you're active duty, you're already employed. If you're recently discharged, simply provide your DD-214 to get your Certificate of Eligibility.

Section 5: Monthly Income and Housing Expense Information

How much money do you make, and how much are you paying for housing now (whether it's rent, mortgage, or living payment-free)? Your income is divided into six sections, plus the now famous "other." Here you enter your base salary, commissions or bonuses, income from investments or dividends, overtime earnings, and any rental income you might have from other real estate. Below this section there is an area for you to describe "other" income. This could be anything that's verifiable, such as child support or alimony payments, note income, or lottery winnings.

Then there is another box for listing your current house payment or rent. Here you put your rent or mortgage payment, plus any monthly property tax, hazard insurance payment, homeowners association dues, or mortgage insurance.

Section 6: Assets and Liabilities

This section covers your bank accounts, investment accounts, IRAs, or whatever other financial assets you might have. Don't let this section intimidate you. Just because there's a space for "Life Insurance Net Cash Value" or "Vested Interest in Retirement Fund" doesn't mean that you have to have either of them to get a home loan. You don't. You simply need enough money to close the deal.

The very first box describes your very first asset involved in the transaction: your "earnest money" or deposit money that you gave along with your sales contract. If you gave $2,000 as earnest money, that's the first money you've put into the deal. The lender wants to know how much you gave as earnest money and who has it, and will verify those funds as part of your down payment.

The next four sections are for listing your bank accounts (checking or savings) and related account information, such as account numbers and current balances. It's not necessary to complete every single box or to divulge every single account you might have. Typically lenders only care about your having enough money to close the deal and less about what your IRA balance is. The only time other balances come into question is if the lender asks for them as a condition of its loan approval. These extra funds are called *reserves*.

Reserves are best described as money left in various accounts after all the dust has settled, including money for your down payment and closing costs. Reserves can sometimes be a multiple of your new house payment, such as "six months worth of housing payments," and they must be in accounts free and clear of your transaction. Reserves can also be used to beef up your application if you're on the border of obtaining a loan approval.

A lender who is a little squishy on a loan may want to see some other aspects of your financial picture before issuing an approval. Reserves are an important criterion for many loans, but it's up to you to ask the lender if you in fact need to document absolutely everything in your financial portfolio or just enough to close the deal.

This section also asks about other real estate you might own, and there is even an area to list the type and value of your car. I'm serious. Again, this is a holdover from earlier loan applications, but if you leave this section blank, an underwriter might want to know how you get to work and back. Finally, there are the "other" assets. Historically, other assets meant expensive artwork or jewelry, but this too is an unnecessary question, so don't worry about leaving this box blank.

Next to assets is the liabilities section, where you list your monthly bills. This section is only for items that might show up on your credit report, such as a car loan or credit card bill. It doesn't include such items as your electricity or telephone bills. Don't worry if you can't remember the exact balances or minimum monthly payment required; just give your best estimate. Your lender will fill the application with correct numbers taken from the credit bureau later on. If you owe child support or alimony, there's a place for that information, too.

Section 7: Details of Transaction

This is the most confusing part of the application, and most borrowers leave it blank for the lender or loan officer to fill in. In fact, most loan officers don't fill it in—they let their computer program do the work for them. This is an overview of your particular deal, showing the sales price of the home, your down payment amount (if any), your closing costs, and any earnest money held anywhere. It then shows how much money you're supposed to bring to the closing table.

Note that this is just an overview and not the final word on the loan amount and costs, etc. It's simply a brief snapshot of the transaction. Believe me, you'll get reams of paper on this topic in other documents.

Section 8: Declarations

These are thirteen statements to which you must answer "yes" or "no." For example, "Are there any outstanding judgments against you?" and "Are you a party to a lawsuit?" and so on. Here you'll also declare if you've been bankrupt or had a foreclosure in the past seven years. Actually, there is no such thing as a seven-year requirement for bankruptcies and foreclosures for conventional or government loans anymore; this is another carryover from older application processes. Nowadays, bankruptcies and foreclosures generally affect loan applications only if they're two to four years old.

Section 9: Acknowledgment and Agreement

This is a long-winded, obviously lawyer-written section where you cross your heart and hope to die that what you put on your application is true, that you agree to have the home secured by a first mortgage or deed of trust, that you won't use the property for illegal purposes, that you didn't lie, and so on. You sign your loan application in this section and date it.

Section 10: Information for Government Monitoring Purposes

This is an optional section that asks about your race, your ethnicity, and whether you are male or female. This information doesn't make any difference on your loan approval and you don't have to fill this out if you don't want. The government requires that when borrowers opt not to complete this information, then the loan officer meeting with the applicants must make a best guess as to "guy or girl" or "black, white, Pacific Islander," or whatever. This is one of the ways the federal government can monitor the approval rates for various classes and races of borrowers. It's called the Home Mortgage Disclosure Act—or HMDA (Hum-duh)—monitoring section. The government uses this information to see if your bank or lender is discriminating based upon race, color, or creed. After all, how does the government know such things if it's not told? Or maybe a certain lender isn't making loans where the community may need them most. For example, the Community Reinvestment Act (CRA) requires lenders to place a certain percentage of their mortgages in underserved areas. This is how the government knows—by requiring such information on loan applications.

Step 3: The Process

After completing all your required paperwork, both from the government and from the lender, it's time to learn what to expect during the process.

First, your loan file is documented by verifying everything you put in your loan application. Verification is done by your loan officer initially, but more likely by your loan processor. You will deliver pay stubs, W-2s, 1099s, bank statements, and any and all third-party verification of your income and assets. We'll discuss the role of the loan officer and loan processor in more detail in Chapter 4.

At this stage, an appraisal, or Notice of Value (NOV), will be ordered to determine the market value of your home. Once the NOV comes in and your property comes in at value, other parts are put together for your home loan.

Your title insurance is issued by a title insurance company. You will contact your homeowners insurance company to get coverage for your home. Your home will be inspected by a home inspector. After jumping these hurdles, your loan file will be transferred to a loan underwriter, or the person who officially "signs off" on the mortgage approval, making sure your loan request complies with VA guidelines.

Once the underwriter approves the loan, it is sent to a closing department that prepares the closing papers for you to sign. Your papers will be printed and then delivered to whomever is handling your closing.

You sign your papers, according to the lenders' instructions, and the papers are sent back to the lender for review. If you've done everything you're supposed to do and the sellers have done everything they're supposed to do, then money changes hands, most typically via an electronic fund transfer called a "wire."

Once funds change hands and all the paperwork is complete, you get the keys and move in.

There, that was easy, wasn't it?

Assumption

One of the more unique features of VA loans is something called "assumption." Assumption means that if someone wanted to buy your home from you, he wouldn't have to find his own financing; he could assume your VA loan that financed the property.

There are two types of assumptions: "qualifying" and "nonqualifying."

Nonqualifying means that anyone, regardless of his or her credit or income history, could simply take over your VA loan . . . no questions asked. This option is only available for VA loans issued prior to March 1, 1988. That's when the VA made certain adjustments to the program. Previously, a loan could simply be transferred from the seller to the buyer without checking a person's credit report or otherwise determining if the buyer of the home had the inclination to pay back the mortgage. Homes were advertised as "VA Nonqualifying Assumable," which would draw typically nonqualified borrowers into home-ownership. The theory behind the practice was to both help the veteran and expand homeownership.

Unfortunately, those who had bad credit continued to have bad credit and began to default on those very same VA loans, sometimes foreclosing on the property altogether.

This situation affected the veteran who transferred the property as well as the lender. If an assumed loan went into foreclosure, the veteran had to pay the difference or he wouldn't be entitled to VA loans anymore.

Then, in 1988, things changed. People who wanted to assume a VA loan would also have to qualify for the new loan just as they would with any other mortgage. They now became "Qualified Assumables."

This new assumable characteristic lost some of its luster because there really was no reason to assume a VA loan unless the loan terms were considerably better on the VA loan than the then-current mortgage market. If a VA loan had a 5.5 percent rate on it and prevailing mortgage rates were in the 7.0 percent range, then it might make sense to assume the VA loan and the low rate that went along with it.

There are also reduced closing fees with assumptions, because lender charges are essentially out of the picture, and there are no appraisal charges or discount points to pay, either.

There are surely some nonqualifying VA loans out there, but not many, as they would have to have been issued some twenty-plus years ago.

CHAPTER 2

Credit and VA Lending

A common misconception about VA lending is that if you've received your Certificate of Eligibility, you're "eligible" and therefore approved. But simply being eligible doesn't mean you get the loan. The VA doesn't lend the money; the VA only guarantees that loan to the lender in case you default. Actually, you help that guarantee in the form of the funding fee (see Chapter 6); but regardless, the VA doesn't issue approvals or denials when you apply for a VA loan.

The lender is the party that approves the loan. Regardless of your Certificate of Eligibility, you still have to qualify, which means you still have to have decent credit. Not necessarily spotless credit, but credit nonetheless.

Establishing Credit

You will have to show the ability to handle your finances, and the lender will want to make sure you can handle a new house payment along with any other monthly payments you're now making. The ability and willingness to repay debt is the way you establish a credit history.

A credit profile is established by you when you borrow money. For example, if you see a car you'd like to have and can't bring in a check for $20,000, you can borrow the money from a lender who will pay the car company. By paying the car lender back when you're supposed to, you're establishing credit.

My favorite way of explaining how credit is established is the "ability and willingness" principle.

When someone has the *ability* to pay back a debt, it means he has the money or other asset to pay back or trade that person what was originally borrowed under the original terms. *Willingness* simply means the inclination to do so.

I recall a story from a client who essentially had messed up his credit. In fact, he was an executive with a major corporation. Not only would you recognize the company he worked for, it's quite possible you would recognize his name.

He contacted me because he needed to refinance his mortgage to pay off some federal tax liens, and he asked me if I could help. "Sure," I said, and sent him a loan application. He completed all the paperwork and returned it to me for review.

I ran his credit report and saw that he had several late payments in addition to the tax liens filed against him. I also looked at his loan application and saw that he had lots of money lying around in various accounts.

He had the "ability" to repay his debts, as evidenced by the money he had in his various accounts, but he was sometimes slow in paying. He didn't have the "willingness" to pay back what was owed. On the other hand, someone can be very eager to repay a debt, even willing to pay off a debt ahead of time, but that person may not have sufficient income or the "ability" to pay off what was originally borrowed.

Ability plus willingness will result in good credit. Both have to be present, as reflected in your payment patterns to your creditors.

Before you can get a loan for that $20,000 car, the car lender will request your payment patterns from a credit repository. There are three main credit repositories: Equifax, TransUnion, and Experian. A repository simply is like a library or database of all credit transactions made by both lenders and borrowers, and it comes in handy because it allows lenders to make decisions more quickly.

Equifax, TransUnion, and Experian report such data electronically to participating business clients. In fact, credit information is requested, transmitted, and evaluated in a matter of seconds. If you've applied for a credit card in the mall or online and gotten a new credit card approved seconds after filling out a credit application, you've just witnessed how credit reporting now works.

That's how you establish credit. You borrow some money or buy something on credit, and then you demonstrate your ability and willingness to pay back that business, because that business reports your timely (or untimely) payment patterns on a routine basis.

By repeating this process you will soon establish a solid credit history. And a solid credit history is perhaps the single most important aspect when defining your financial future. Your ability to borrow at competitive rates and leverage your income will have a positive impact on your life. You will be able to retire sooner, with more money, and with a big ol' smile on your face.

Credit and the Armed Forces

First and foremost, the armed forces has trained you to make good credit choices, and you know how having a bad credit profile is not only bad for you personally but could be a detriment to the safety of the United States. Bad credit means you could lose assignments. If you've got money problems at home and get deployed, the brass knows there's an increased likelihood that you'll be trying to find more money than your actual pay. That situation could lead some people to sell stuff they shouldn't be selling, or tell stuff they shouldn't be telling, just to make some extra money. That's a security risk.

Having money problems also means that when you're deployed or, for that matter, when you're functioning in any capacity for the United States of America, you're not giving your full mental devotion to your prescribed activity. If your job is disarming explosive devices or transporting other troops, then it's vitally important that you're focusing 100 percent on your job and not wondering if the credit card company is going to send you to collection. Should your mind wander, you could endanger people and property.

If your job is clerical and you make a mistake because you're thinking about your bills instead of mentally concentrating on your job, then you're guilty of having credit problems that control your working life. Yes, it happens to civvies, too, but their jobs are not national security—yours is.

Career military? Bad credit? Your promotions will be on the line. If you have bad credit or get yourself into a bad credit situation, it could cause you to make bad decisions to repay those debts. Good credit and good service to your country go hand in hand. Enough said.

What If You Don't Have a Credit History?

If you don't have credit, the best place to start might be at a department store such as Sears or Target. Department stores are more lenient when it comes to offering credit to those seeking credit for the first time. And it's not limited to those stores. Most any store offering its own credit card may be willing to "take a chance" on you and be the first to issue a credit card to you.

Of course, the credit limit on new department-store accounts will be low. If you have no credit profile at all, don't expect a $10,000 credit line at JCPenney. Instead, you can anticipate something along the lines of a $250 or $500 limit, for starters.

But only apply for one account, charge something on it, and pay it off. Don't apply for several accounts at once, because that could indicate you're relying on credit instead of trying to build a credit history. Choose an account that you would normally and regularly use, such as a service station account. Service station accounts are also easy to apply and get approved for if you have no credit. Or buy something you would otherwise need, but instead of paying cash for it, charge it to the new credit account. If you need a new washer and dryer, try opening up a new store credit account, then pay it off each month as it comes due.

After a certain period—say, within six to twelve months of timely payment—you'll one day open up your account statement and see that your credit limit has been increased . . . all because you demonstrated the ability and willingness to repay your debts.

Organizations That Hurt Credit

There are places that you want to avoid when trying to establish a credit rating. First, "rent to own" companies do little, if anything, to help your credit. In fact, you'll be charged much higher interest rates from such firms than if you borrowed the money on a new credit card account. Second, rent-to-own companies are likely not to report your payment patterns to the credit bureaus.

Instead of paying stratospheric interest rates for cheap equipment or furnishings for your apartment or house, try saving up for a few months instead, then apply those savings as a down payment on a credit account. For example, say you wanted to buy a new or used stereo. Instead of going to a rent-to-own business, hold off for a few more months (hey, you got along this far without it, didn't you?), save that money, then buy the stereo with some down payment as well as credit. The money you saved in interest charges on rent-to-own arrangements is money earned. It's yours.

Stay away, too, from payday loan companies. Payday loans are loans made to individuals who sign a draft or postdate a check for the amount borrowed plus a fee. On payday, the draft is issued and the funds are deducted from the borrower's account. These fees are stifling, sometimes as much as $20 per each $100 borrowed, and when annualized, the result is an interest rate hovering near 500 percent. Payday loan companies will rip you off, and they won't report your "loan" to any credit bureau.

There are other companies that beg for your credit-improvement business. Firms that advertise as "E-Z Credit" or "Build Your Credit Here" can only serve to harm your credit profile.

Credit Scores

Understanding the basics of credit reporting is the key to building your future. Understanding how credit scores are calculated is equally important. That's right. Credit scores. They are a new entry in credit reporting.

Credit scoring is an attempt to assign a numerical value to a credit profile. Developed several years ago by Fair Isaac Corporation, or FICO, this system helps to streamline the credit approval process. Instead of a lender reviewing a credit report line item by line item, the lender would instead look at the number assigned to that individual's report.

Credit scores can range from as low as 300 to as high as 850. The higher the number, the better the credit. An "average" credit score is around 680, while anything above 720 would be considered "excellent" and anything below 600 could be considered "damaged" or "poor" credit.

When you hear people talking about credit scores, this is what they're talking about. One thing VA loans do not do is require a certain credit score to be approved; nonetheless, credit scores are an integral piece of the approval process.

Before you apply for any mortgage loan you should first check your credit report for both errors and omissions. You can get a free annual credit report by visiting www.annualcreditreport.com or by writing to:

Annual Credit Report Request Service
P.O. Box 105281
Atlanta, GA 30348

Correcting Mistakes on Credit Reports

Mistakes can happen, and with credit reports they occur more than they should. They happen for a variety of reasons, but one of the most common is because of similar names. If your name is Joe Smith, then you can bet there are a lot of Joe Smiths out there. When a business reports Joe Smith's payment history to the credit bureaus, that information can get mistakenly assigned to the other Joe Smiths in the system.

When companies report credit histories, they don't merely send in someone's name, they also attach where the consumer lives, the person's Social Security number, and other identifying information. You would think that should help prevent Joe Smith who lives in Seattle from having his credit information erroneously applied to Joe Smith who lives in Miami. Alas, mistakes still occur.

When you're applying for a mortgage, at the very least you need to be aware of mistakes. More important, you want any mistakes fixed before a lender sees your loan. Yes, mistakes can be fixed after you apply for a home loan; it just takes longer to get them fixed. And if something holds up your loan application, it's possible you'll go past the closing date on your house, losing out to someone else who wants to buy it. Even a few days can affect a closing.

How do you fix mistakes? By providing written documentation of the error. A common mistake in credit reporting is late payments. When you open up your credit card statement, you'll see a "due date" listed. You're supposed to pay on or before that date. Credit reporting agencies don't report if you're a little beyond that due date, but they do report if you're more than thirty days past the due date, as well as sixty days, ninety days, and 120 days past due.

If, after reviewing your credit report, you see that a late payment has been reported and you disagree with that reporting, you'll need to dig up some canceled checks or payment receipts proving that your payment was in fact not late. A common misconception is that if you disagree with something in the report, all you need to do is write a letter to the credit bureau disputing that late payment. Not the case. A credit bureau will accept your dispute letter and keep it in your file, but it will not erase the late payment simply because of your letter. Nope, you have to provide third-party evidence that you were on time.

If, however, you provide copies of your check clearing before the due date or show a receipt of payment before the due date, then the credit bureau will remove the negative item. Not only will that bureau remove the item, but by law it must notify the other two bureaus of the mistake. If TransUnion is reporting a late payment and you prove that the report is incorrect, TransUnion must also contact Equifax and Experian and have them remove the mistake as well.

The most efficient way of getting mistakes corrected is to solicit the help of your loan officer at the mortgage company. In fact, a good loan officer can get mistakes corrected in a matter of minutes instead of the thirty to sixty days it might take a consumer to accomplish the very same thing.

Credit reporting agencies have customers. No, not you, but the lenders who use them to get credit data. Those credit agencies are just like any other business in that they have customer service representatives or salespeople who do nothing but make calls to their customers to make sure they're happy. Are customers getting reports on time? Are their telephone calls or e-mails answered promptly, and so on? The credit reporting business is fiercely competitive. After all, the credit agencies are all working with the very same data. So they have to offer different, special, or otherwise superior service that their competitors can't or won't match.

One of these services is correcting mistakes on their customers' credit reports.

If you're applying for a VA loan and a mistake pops up on your credit report, your loan officer can provide a paid statement and clear title, fax it directly to her credit account representative, and within a few hours the mistake is corrected. (If you tried to do it yourself, it would be a nightmare just trying to deal with the bureaucracy.) A mortgage company may not even need to correct anything on the credit report if the collection account is relatively minor compared to your entire credit profile and you provide third-party documentation of the error.

But what if it's not a mistake? What if you can't back up your claim or otherwise dispute the information being reported? The Equal Credit Opportunity Act, or ECOA, allows you to write a letter to the reporting bureaus telling your side of the story.

If there's a dispute, you can write an explanation letter, but that's not going to have any effect on a credit score. You can write a narrative of what happened and mail, e-mail, or fax it in. But so what? Because mortgage companies no longer manually review a credit report, the letter isn't reviewed by the potential lender. You may have one of the coolest explanation letters ever composed, but your potential mortgage company couldn't care less. That may sound harsh, but the reality is that explanation letters carry little, if any, weight in the new world of credit reports.

You also want to review your credit report to see if there is something that should be in it but isn't. If you've opened up a credit card account or gotten an automobile loan, it's possible that information isn't showing up on your report. If you've made your payments on time, then this information is important to keep your credit score up. If you have an account that is not reporting to the credit bureaus, call the company issuing the loan or credit and ask that it report your timely payment history to the three bureaus.

Once you get your mistakes fixed and your omissions reported, you can continue on your home loan journey knowing that your credit habits are being reported in the best possible light.

Creating a Good Credit History

VA loans are a bit more lenient when it comes to credit standards, but by no means are they designed for people carrying negative credit profiles. If you've got bad credit, you need to fix it. And the best way to fix it is knowing how to establish good credit in the first place.

A positive credit profile is established by:

- Never being more than thirty days late on an account

- Not going above the credit limits issued

- Keeping your balances low compared with your credit limits

When you open up a credit account, you're given your terms: how much you can borrow, at what interest rate, and when your payments are due. How much you can borrow is your *credit limit*. If you open up a credit card account and you can charge no more than $2,000, then $2,000 is your limit.

If you ever go over your credit limit, your credit score will be hurt. But if your limit is $2,000, then how can you go over it? Good question. Typically it happens when you charge the maximum and let your interest charges get added up on top of your limit. Even if you go over the limit one day and immediately pay it down the next day, the damage has already been done.

Next to the credit limit in importance is how much you should charge compared with your credit limit. One of the best ways to establish excellent credit is to keep your *loan balance* right at one-third of your limit. This is sometimes called your "available credit," and it is expressed as a percentage.

If your credit limit is $10,000 and your ideal balance is one-third of that, then try to keep a balance somewhere near $3,330. But wait, isn't a zero balance better? No, it's not. Not for building a solid credit history as reflected by your credit scores. Credit scores improve when you can show that not only will you borrow money and not abuse it by tapping your entire credit limit, but that you also have the inclination to pay it back when it's due.

How can lenders determine creditworthiness if you never borrow anything? They can't really, so that's where the available-balance number comes into play. But an interesting twist occurs when applying this practice, and it involves open versus closed accounts.

It was long held that closing credit lines no longer used was a good practice of someone having a strong credit report, and for two reasons. First, the longer an unused account is kept open, the greater the chance that someone can steal the credit card. Second, closing old accounts is a responsible thing to do so people won't be tempted to start charging stuff they don't need.

That's still good advice, but because credit scores have replaced a manual credit review by a human being, it is the scores themselves that are most important, and they are affected significantly by two factors: on-time payments and available balances. Closing down an account due to nonuse can actually have a negative effect on your credit. Why?

Credit scores increase when you're on time with your payments and keep your balances within 30 percent of your limits. For instance, you have three credit cards, each with a $10,000 credit line. So your total credit line is $30,000. Ideally, at least from a credit score perspective, you would have 30 percent of those credit lines charged, or $10,000.

Now let's say you transfer balances from two of those cards and put them on one card. That leaves you with two cards with no balances, so you close those accounts. Two things happen: Suddenly, your credit card account is now at your new available limit, or $10,000. Being at your limit hurts your score. Also, and worse yet, you are now at 100 percent of your available credit: $10,000 limit and a $10,000 balance. After just a few weeks, your credit will begin to deteriorate.

However, if you had left those three accounts alone, you would have the optimal credit scenario—available credit at 30 percent of your allowable limits and on-time payments. Your scores will soon zoom into the 800s.

This formula works with any available credit limit. If you have $3,000 available credit, keep that balance as close to $1,000 as long as you can, and don't be late on your payments. The amount of the credit line doesn't matter as much as the relationship between your credit balances and your limits.

If you're just starting to build a credit profile, it's good advice to try and establish at least three credit lines as soon as you're able. You'll likely start with one card, then soon another, and finally another. Charge something, get a balance, then begin paying it on time when due.

But resist the urge to go overboard and charge more. Credit to some people can be a burden. They think, "Hey, I'll charge it now then pay it off over time," which is fine. But if too much credit is used and more and more accounts are opened, then you could soon find yourself in a bad situation, harming all the hard work you did to establish a good credit profile in the first place.

Get three accounts and don't open up any more.

Negative Credit Ratings

You can also get a negative credit rating from the types of credit accounts you open. Specifically, this is a warning about accounts from finance companies that are recognized in the business as catering to people with financial difficulties. When credit is issued to you by one of these credit firms, your credit score will reflect it and penalize you for borrowing money from a firm with high rates. People will usually borrow at high rates only when they have to, indicating they could be in a tough financial situation.

Now you know how to repair bad credit. It's establishing good credit. By knowing what makes for a good score, you also know how to repair credit that has been hurt.

First, pay off any collection accounts or other seriously outstanding items on your report. Of course, make certain those collections are legitimate, but the longer you take to pay those off, the longer those items remain. You can't begin to repair your credit until you take care of the bad stuff first.

Second, pay down those credit lines. Add up all your credit limits then add up all your balances and compare the differences. Do your balances add up to 80 percent of your available credit? 85 percent? 95 percent? Or more?

It will be very intimidating at first. Perhaps impossible to do. After all, it probably took years to accumulate that debt and you're probably struggling to pay it every month. But instead of trying to pay them all off at the same time, choose the one with your highest balance and highest rate. This is far more effective than just paying on this card and that card. Instead, focus on paying down the one that's charging you the most money each month. After you've knocked that balance down to 30 percent of its limit, work on the next highest balance account. Then the next, and so on.

One key aspect of a credit score is that it's a reflection of your most recent two-year period. So any positive change you begin making will sooner, rather than later, affect your credit score. Any positive change you make in your credit profile by paying down a balance, paying off a collection account, or making your payments on time will yield a positive result sooner than you think.

Negative items on your credit report from years ago reflect your credit behavior years ago, not necessarily now. Or at least in your recent past. When people have experienced bad credit but repaired it, the credit profile is given new life, giving someone a brand-new start.

Keeping a good credit rating simply means continuing to do the very same things that got you there. Sometimes, though, people with newfound "credit wealth" let it get to their heads and not their pocket-books.

I recall a student several years ago who got her first credit card offer in the mail. "You're Preapproved!" it said. So she completed the application, and a couple of weeks later her brand-new card appeared. Soon, a few other offers came in, one from a department store and another from a gasoline company.

She was set. She used the service station card when she needed gas and paid her accounts on time. She really didn't need anything from the department store, but one time she did want a new washer and dryer, so she used her new card to charge it. And she paid it back on time.

This went on for a couple of years, and one day she saw me about buying a new home. She didn't have anything picked out but wanted to get preapproved before she went house shopping. We took her credit application and ran her credit report, and she was floored when she saw that her credit score was in the high 700 range. Excellent credit, I told her.

But what happened next is not so uncommon. Knowing that she had a fantastic credit score, she applied for other credit lines from merchants that were all too happy to issue new plastic. After all, she had been responsible in the past and was being rewarded for it. But she changed her credit patterns.

She suddenly began buying things she didn't need or paid for everyday items with her credit cards. She charged more than she should have, approaching her maximum limits from time to time. But, hey, she always paid on time, right? And credit card companies love that. They also love higher interest rates. Especially if the consumer pays those higher rates on time, as expected.

After a few months of house shopping, she began to get serious about making an offer on a home. She then contacted me, telling me just that, and asked that I get her preapproval letter ready. Because it had been a while since I reviewed her credit, I pulled it again. Big problem: Her credit scores had dropped. Significantly.

Not only had she opened up multiple lines of new credit, she had also "maxed out" several of those cards, paying only the minimum each month. Now her score had been lowered, her credit card payments had gone up, and her subsequent mortgage rate had been increased. Only about 0.25 percent, but an increase nonetheless. On a $250,000 loan, a 0.25 percent increase in rate means nearly a $15,000 difference on a thirty-year mortgage. That's a lot.

She was shocked. Just six months earlier she had one of the best credit scores around. But not anymore. In fact, she had damaged her credit in the most severe of ways: She charged too much, opened up too many new accounts, and paid late.

If she had only continued to do the things she did that got the excellent credit in the first place, she would have had every mortgage option available to her. But she didn't. Many people probably would have taken the higher-rate loan. Not her. The credit-score drop slapped her in the face and she took it hard. She straightened up her act, decided not to buy at that time, and spent the next six months trying to get her credit back in shape.

Could she have simply bought at a slightly higher rate? Sure. No big deal. Could rates have actually gone up while she was repairing her credit? Again, yeah. But it was personal with her. She took it upon herself to make amends and fix what needed to be fixed. I admired her for that.

Can you repair your credit by having someone who is not your spouse co-borrow with you, if that person has good credit? No, not with a VA loan, unless the person is also an eligible veteran. Okay, he or she doesn't have to be an eligible veteran, but if not, then the person is underwritten as a nonveteran. In that case, you suddenly need a down payment, because that's what that person would need for a conventional loan, which means no VA loan for either of you.

Are there any shortcuts to repairing credit?

You might think so by searching the Internet for credit repair firms or reading newspaper advertisements: "Credit Repair Made Easy" or "Erase Bad Credit!"

Don't fall for it. Scam city, baby. Okay, I'll take part of that back. There might be companies out there that charge you money to repair your credit, but they're simply doing the things you can do yourself. And they charge you money for the privilege. But it's still a scam.

How do these "companies" perform such miracles? Actually, there are no miracles. But usually the scam, er, routine, works like this: You send in money to them, up-front, of course. They either run your credit report or you supply one for them. They look for mistakes, which is something you can do. Then, if there are mistakes, they ask you for third-party documentation to verify those mistakes.

"Were you really late on that car payment? Can you provide us a statement and copy of a canceled check showing that you in fact were not late?" Sound familiar?

One credit repair scam asks that you establish a brand-new credit profile with a new Social Security number. Or perhaps even a new name. If you're Mr. Smith with your very own Social Security number, then perhaps you can apply for a new Social Security number under the name Big Bad Smith. Or maybe you can change your name entirely to Little Good Jones. And get a new identity. This is one way some of these firms get you your very own "New Credit Profile!"

The gig is to get a new credit application with a different name and Social Security number and begin your credit life all anew. It will take some time, probably a couple of years before some merchant will find you and offer you a new account. Many times, though, those same credit repair companies also happen to know other companies that will extend you credit in some capacity and then report your credit patterns to the three main bureaus. Voila! Brand-new credit.

Everything is so far on the up-and-up, but the premise is bad. There's a lie to begin with.

On the mortgage loan application, there is a specific question that asks, "Have you been known by any other name?" It is easy enough to understand why that question is there. Now you're in a real catch-22. If you have altered your name and Social Security number to hide your bad credit past, and if you lie and say, "No, I have not been known by any other name," then you've just committed loan fraud. Or, you answer, "Yes, I have been known by another name," and your bad credit past is revealed. There is no way to legally change your identity in order to qualify for a home loan by lying about and trying to cover up your past.

This becomes an issue when your loan gets audited or there is a payment default. There is a form that most every mortgage loan requires, and it's called the IRS Form 4506. This is an authorization form that lenders ask you to sign, giving them the authority to check with the Internal Revenue Service to compare what you put on your loan application to what has been reported to the IRS in the past. If you put down on your loan application that you made $5,000 per month, the 4506 form allows a lender to independently verify that information with the IRS, and long after your mortgage loan is closed.

Another instance where your loan application is audited is when there's a foreclosure on the property or during a "first payment default." During a foreclosure proceeding, a lender will determine, among other things, that you did or did not lie on your loan application. When it's found out that you were known as Big Dog Smith as well as Little Cat Jones, you're guilty of loan fraud.

Mortgage loan fraud is a big-time offense. Money can cross state lines, making it a federal crime. Lying on a mortgage application is serious business. It's not a slap on the wrist. It's time in the big house. Or the brig. Or whatever. But it hurts. And it's not worth lying on an application solely to buy property.

So, in this instance, when or if you have changed your identity, you're eventually going to be caught.

Credit Counseling Services

Another instance of credit repair revolves around credit counseling services. Credit counseling services can be a good thing. They can also be a bad thing.

Counseling services charge you a fee to renegotiate your credit obligations with your creditors, setting up new monthly payment structures and putting you on the path to credit repair. Not bad, but you have to be careful with such companies.

Credit counseling companies typically work this way: They negotiate new, favorable terms for you, and you pay the counseling company a fee for setting up the new arrangements. You pay the counseling company money each month, whereby the company distributes those funds to your creditors. When you have paid off all the creditors after your payment schedule has been met, your credit accounts should read "Paid in full."

Why would credit card companies agree to do such a thing?

Credit card companies often recognize the credit counseling offer as an attempt to pay debt back before the consumer files for bankruptcy completely, denying the credit company any income at all . . . and forcing it to write off the balance altogether. A credit counseling offer is usually an in-lieu payment compared to a complete write-off of the debt to the creditor. And it can also mean the consumer isn't filing for bankruptcy but instead is making an effort to pay back the debts.

After you've paid these accounts, typically those accounts will be closed by the credit grantor and will be noted as such in your credit report. But not always. It's possible that those same credit grantors want to keep your credit account and let you begin charging again— assuming, of course, that you've paid your current balance below the limit and you're current on those accounts. It's their call.

However, it's very important to note that sometimes these counseling agencies don't always act in your best interest. They may attempt to, but often they don't.

When the counseling agency negotiates new terms with one of your credit card companies, the scenario may play out something like this:

"Hi, this is Credit Counseling Company, and we have been hired by Big Dog Smith to structure a new payment schedule with you. Big Dog owes $10,000 with you and is paying $400 per month at 33 percent interest. We are willing to offer you a new plan, reducing the interest rate to zero for twelve months and also dropping the balance owed to $5,000. We'd like to know if you'd be interested."

The creditor is now thinking, "Okay, this girl is getting ready to file bankruptcy, so let's try and get some of our money back." So the creditor might agree to the new terms, saying, "Alright, just send us $100 per month for twelve months and we'll drop the balance owed to $8,000," or something like that.

The counseling service repeats this offer with all your creditors. Now, instead of sending money to every one of your creditors, you instead send one lump sum to the counseling service, which distributes it.

Or at least it's supposed to. Once money passes from you to the service, you have no control over when your creditors are being paid. If it's late, you're late . . . regardless of when you sent in your money.

That can compound the problem. Even if you've been successful at renegotiating your debt obligations, being late on them or otherwise reneging on the whole arrangement will accelerate collection and court efforts, which can result in judgments.

It's something to consider and, quite frankly, look at carefully. It may be better to negotiate directly with your creditors and not pay some third-party company to do what you could have done otherwise, on your own and under your control.

Impact of a Bankruptcy

When people get into credit trouble, they can get embarrassed. "I am not worthy," they think. I can relate. I've been there. Many moons ago, but I've been there. It's not fun. But if you've got bad credit or need some help, you need to stop with the "Why me?" routine, strap your boots on, and take care of the problem.

Bad credit happens when bad things happen, such as a loss of job or a divorce. When (not if) those things happen to people, those who prepare for disasters are more easily able to weather any credit storm that might arise.

But what if something bad does happen to you and you're not able to pay your bills any longer? Federal law allows you to discharge those debts through bankruptcy protection.

Bankruptcy is nothing to be taken lightly. In fact, if you're thinking about filing for bankruptcy, the first place you need to go is to a bankruptcy lawyer for legal advice. A bankruptcy lawyer can help answer all your questions and let you know the impact a bankruptcy will have.

There are two types of bankruptcy protection: Chapter 7 and Chapter 13.

Chapter 13 is sometimes called the "wage earners" plan because it doesn't completely wipe out any debt but instead simply rearranges that debt into a more manageable load. But not everyone has a choice in how to file. In 2005, bankruptcy laws were changed dramatically, and not necessarily in favor of the consumer.

It used to be that if a consumer wanted to file for bankruptcy, she would decide on her own if she wanted to pay anyone back at all or simply wipe out all her revolving and installment debt completely, getting a brand-new start by choosing to file a Chapter 7 or Chapter 13.

Now, however, a consumer doesn't have a "choice," but instead has a test she needs to go through. This test is actually an income limit that she must be at or below. If her income is at or below the median income levels for her area, she can choose a complete discharge via a Chapter 7 filing or a repayment plan using a Chapter 13. If her income is above the median income for her area, then she has no choice and instead works out a payment schedule with her trustee to pay everyone back.

But what if you're unemployed? Doesn't that automatically mean you're below the median income because you don't have any income? Nope. The new bankruptcy laws will use your previous six months' average income regardless of your current employment or income status.

Under a Chapter 13, you add up all your bills and present that amount to a court-appointed trustee. The trustee will then choose a repayment period from two to five years to pay everyone back. The principal amounts owed to the various creditors will be added up, and the trustee will look at your available cash (meaning cash on hand after paying housing, taxes, insurance, food, and other "living" expenses) and divide what's owed by the amount available each month to pay.

Under a Chapter 7, nothing of the sort occurs. Everything you owe is wiped off the books.

From a mortgage-qualifying standpoint, which looks better on your credit report, the Chapter 13 or the Chapter 7? Oddly, neither is more favorable. In fact, a case can be made that a Chapter 13 is worse than a Chapter 7 as it relates to a credit score.

Credit repair can't begin until the bad stuff is finished. And mortgage lenders pay special attention to the *discharge date* of a bankruptcy, which is the date when the bankruptcy is officially completed.

Recall that a credit history relies most heavily on a consumer's most recent two-year period. Under a Chapter 7, two years later, credit will gradually begin to improve, provided the consumer didn't start making late payments again. But under a Chapter 13 filing, there is still an active bankruptcy on the credit report, and the two-year discharge date will not have started until way past when the Chapter 7 was discharged.

Under a Chapter 7, a consumer could have begun reestablishing credit during those two years while someone under a Chapter 13 would still have an active bankruptcy, perhaps with even three more years to go. A Chapter 13 may not see any significant credit repair up until seven years have passed, if the Chapter 13 repayment period was five years plus two years' recovery period.

But is there another option? What about consumer credit counseling services?

Although they're certainly an option, despite their sometimes lack of accountability, they're actually viewed the same as a bankruptcy. It's true. From a pure mortgage-lender standpoint, consumer credit agencies may be just as harmful to a credit report as a Chapter 7 or Chapter 13 bankruptcy.

A common myth is that lenders won't make a mortgage loan with a bankruptcy on the credit report, or that you have to wait ten years for the bankruptcy to finally remove itself from the report. Not true in any sense.

Interestingly enough, VA loans have more lenient credit guidelines in this regard. Although a nongovernment loan will typically require that four years must pass from the time of the bankruptcy discharge before a mortgage loan can be issued, VA loans are more forgiving, allowing for only twenty-four months to pass before issuing a mortgage after a bankruptcy. Not bad, huh?

If you've got a recent bankruptcy in your past and qualify for a VA loan, this is truly a benefit. That's because nongovernment loans for a bankruptcy less than four years old are reserved for subprime lenders, or lenders who specialize in loans for those with damaged credit. We'll discuss subprime lending later, in Chapter 8, but such loans always carry much higher interest rates than what VA loans offer.

Foreclosures

Foreclosures mean the borrower couldn't or didn't pay back the lender and the lender took the house back. Most often, foreclosure proceedings begin after three successive payments have been missed.

It's an intense ordeal. It's the method of last resort for most homeowners, and it's also the last resort for lenders. Lenders aren't in the business of foreclosing on properties. It means either the lender made a mistake in issuing a mortgage loan in the first place or something bad happened after the loan was first issued, such as a loss of job, illness, or death in the family.

If there is a foreclosure in your past, the VA won't consider issuing a new VA loan if the foreclosed loan was a previous VA loan of your own. Yes, the funding fee helped pay for that bad debt, but if there's a VA foreclosure in your past, then you'll need to look elsewhere for financing.

On the other hand, if you have a foreclosure in your past and it wasn't a VA loan, and as long as it's been three years since the foreclosure, then the VA can allow for such a thing to have happened, given other positive credit criteria, of course.

You don't want to risk a foreclosure, so the first thing you should do is try and avoid it in the first place. I know that sounds easy, but what it really means is that you need to contact the lender before you get a couple of months behind on your mortgage payments and explain what's going on.

It costs lenders lots of money to foreclose. They have to pay lawyers. There are back taxes that have to be paid, along with lost interest, the costs of selling the home and fixing it up . . . so the lender is already behind. If a lender forecloses too often, that lender won't be in business too long.

When you call your lender, explain the situation you're in. You typically have a few options. One would be to take the amount you are behind on, divide it up, then spread it out over the next few months, typically three to six months. If your monthly payment is $1,200 and you've missed two payments in a row, the lender might ask that you take that $2,400, divide it into six equal installments, then add that amount to your next six house payments. For the next six months your payment would be $1,600 instead of $1,200.

There are also laws that require lenders to help you avoid foreclosure in the form of a "workaround," which will examine your new financial situation with regard to income and current total debt load, then work out smaller monthly payment while you get back on your feet.

But again, don't hide from the situation. Yeah, bad credit can be embarrassing, and perhaps you feel a little shell-shocked and find yourself doing nothing. Resist that urge, pick up the phone, and begin some dialogue. Believe me, both you and your lender will breathe a sigh of relief.

If in the end you can't make your payments and you find yourself in foreclosure, you'll typically get a certified letter from an attorney letting you know there's pending litigation on you called a *lis pendens*. You'll never call it that, but that's what it's called.

You will be given the opportunity to reinstate your mortgage before the home goes up for sale at an auction . . . usually within forty-five to six days or so, depending on how often those auctions take place where you live. The amount of money will be what you've missed in payments, plus some attorneys' fees, plus your next house payment. It's a lot, but at this point, that's where you stand.

If you can't make those payments yet you still want to keep your house, you'll need to find an attorney to help you, primarily to file for bankruptcy protection while you get your physical and financial houses in order.

And there won't be any lack of legal resources available to you, much less other options. Because a foreclosure notice is a legal proceeding, it's public. There are companies that specialize in selling foreclosure data to other businesses with some business interest in the foreclosure process.

You'll get letters and postcards from real estate agents who either want to buy your home from you or list it before it goes into foreclosure. You'll get letters and postcards from individuals who want to buy your house. You'll get letters and postcards from attorneys offering their assistance. And you'll keep getting those letters and postcards until the foreclosure proceedings have stopped, one way or another.

The key here is to avoid foreclosure altogether. When you find yourself in a financial bind, let your lender know about it as early as possible. Lenders are very forgiving when they know you're trying to work with them. If you don't answer their telephone calls or letters asking you why you haven't paid your mortgage, it makes them nervous and could cause them to think you don't really want to keep the home.

CHAPTER 3

The VA Loan Approval Process

Now that you've gotten your paperwork in order with your Certificate of Eligibility in your hands, it's time to go shopping for a home. Er, wait. Maybe not. Maybe you should find out what you can afford first.

Knowing how much a lender will loan you is different from what the VA will guarantee to a lender. If a lender will issue a maximum VA loan of $417,000, that doesn't mean that's how much you're going to borrow. Nope, it's only a limit. What you can afford and what is available can be two entirely different things.

For instance, although you may be able to afford a $5,000-per-month mortgage, it's not available from a VA lender. That $5,000 per month works to a loan amount of somewhere near $600,000, which is way above a VA lender's maximum VA loan. Of course, there's the other scenario as well: Although a $417,000 loan is available, your debt ratio may suggest a more modest loan amount is in store for you.

Lenders will determine how much you can borrow by looking at how much you make every month and comparing it with what your current and future monthly payments will be. Your total monthly payments divided by your gross monthly income is called your *debt ratio*.

If your total monthly payments are $2,000 and your gross monthly income is $6,000, then your qualifying VA ratio is $2,000 / $6,000 or 0.33, or 33 percent. The maximum qualifying VA ratio stands at 41, meaning that the most a VA loan will allow for your monthly obligations compared to your gross income is 41 percent.

So, in this example, 41 percent of $6,000 is $2,460. That $2,460 must include your house payment and any other monthly bills you might have—monthly bills that would appear on your credit report, that is.

Monthly payments are divided into two categories: housing and everything else. Let's say you find a $250,000 home and rates are 6.50 percent for a thirty-year fixed-rate VA loan. That works out to $1,572 per month for principal and interest. For purposes of calculating debt ratios, a lender will also include in that housing payment one-twelfth of your annual homeowners insurance premium and one-twelfth of your annual property tax bill.

If your homeowners insurance premium is $1,250 on a $250,000 house, then one-twelfth of $1,250 is $104. If your property taxes are $2,000 per year, then one-twelfth of $2,000 is $167. By adding $1,572 to the $104 for insurance and $167 for property taxes, you get $1,843 in principal, interest, taxes, and insurance—what's most commonly called PITI.

Now divide $1,843 by your gross income of $6,000 and your ratio is $1,843/$6,000, or 31 percent. But wait, you have a few other bills that need to be calculated in this equation. A car payment of $300, a credit card payment of $50, a cable television bill of $59, an electric bill of $85, and a student loan payment of $75. But some of these monthly payments count toward your debt ratio and some do not. Which ones do not?

Generally, if the monthly payment does not appear on a credit report, it's not used to calculate ratios. Electricity bills, cell phone bills, dog grooming, or any other "utility" item isn't counted. But if it appears on the credit report, it is.

Remember that businesses report to credit reporting agencies so that they can more easily make lending decisions. Your telephone bill doesn't report to the credit bureau, at least not unless you decided to never pay your telephone bill again for the rest of your life and the phone company sent you to a collection agency for nonpayment.

In this example, only the car payment, the credit card payment, and the student loan would be used to calculate debt ratios, leaving everything else out of the picture.

By adding those three items to the PITI, you get closer to a total debt-to-income ratio. So, $300 plus $50 plus $75 added to the PITI of $1,843 equals $2,268. And $2,268 divided by $6,000 is 38 percent. Your ratio is 38.

What happens when your ratios are over 41? What happens if your car payment is $800 (because you have two cars), plus $1,000 minimum credit card payments, plus student loans totaling $300 per month? By adding everything together with the original $1,843 PITI, the total debt load is $3,943. Your debt ratio, then, is:

$$\$3,943 / \$6,000 = 65.7 \text{ percent, or } 66$$

That's way above the 41 percent guideline set by VA lenders.

Would you be declined a loan if you had a 66 ratio? Probably. What about a 42? Is 42 too high? No, it's not. The 41 qualifying ratio is only a guideline, not a hard-and-fast rule. But just a few short years ago, if your ratios were above 41, you would have had to provide some pretty good answers as to why an underwriter should approve you for a higher loan amount than what the VA ratio suggests.

An underwriter is a person at a mortgage company who reviews your loan file to make sure you fit the guidelines the VA requires. Because the 41 ratio is a VA staple, the underwriter will add up your debt and monthly payments to make sure your ratio is at or below 41.

If the underwriter determines that, yes, you fit the VA loan requirements, you get your approval. If your ratio was above 41—say, 43, 44, or 45—then the underwriter could decline the loan application. And it's not because she's being mean. If the VA loan ever went into foreclosure and the debt ratios were above 41, then the underwriter would have a lot of explaining to do about her decision: "Well, the reason I approved this loan even though the debt ratios were a little high was that the borrower had just graduated from college and the co-borrower just got a promotion," or some such explanation.

Underwriters get hired and fired for making good or bad underwriting decisions. And when a loan goes bad, the underwriter can get a bad reputation for approving loans that shouldn't be approved.

Because manual underwriting carries such personal risks, underwriters would be reluctant to provide any leeway whatsoever, just to keep their jobs safe. Sure, one of their main jobs is to approve loans, but the other side of the coin is making sure they don't approve loans that have no business being approved.

VA Guarantees

One note about VA loan guarantees: If a lender approves a VA loan and it goes bad, as long as the VA loan was underwritten completely by VA guidelines, the VA reimburses the lender for the amount of your original guarantee.

If, however, it is determined that the lender made a VA-guaranteed loan but didn't follow all the VA guidelines, such as approving someone with a 45 ratio and not a 41, then the VA doesn't have to guarantee that loan. The lender would have to foreclose and lose out entirely on the VA guaranty. That's why underwriters can be "mean."

Another advancement in the home loan process has replaced most manual underwriting procedures. This advancement is called an Automated Underwriting System, or AUS.

An AUS is actually a software program that takes all the loan data and issues, within minutes, a loan approval. The loan data is all the information taken from the original five-page Fannie Mae Form 1003, plus the credit report.

When you apply for a VA loan, the lender inputs all your information into the mortgage software program. If you applied online, the lender simply downloads your application directly onto his computer. Once the application is in the computer, the lender then checks the application for errors or other mistakes, such as a Social Security number that doesn't have enough numbers in it, or an incomplete property address, and so on.

The lender then pushes a "send" button on the computer and, within a few moments, the loan application is either approved or not approved. Ratios are reviewed, assets are addressed, and credit is pulled from the bureaus. Voila! Instant loan approval.

In this fashion, if a ratio is above 41 (say, 43, 44, 45, or even higher) and a loan approval is issued by the AUS, and if the loan ever goes bad, then the lender is protected because the approval was issued by the previously approved method of the AUS.

An AUS also has other advantages besides being simply quicker. It allows for the loan officer at the mortgage company to "adjust" the loan application for an approval. This may sound like you're tricking the system into issuing an approval when none is deserved, but what it really means is that if the veteran applies for a $210,000 loan and doesn't get an approval via the AUS, then the loan officer can try again with another loan amount—say, a bit lower at $200,000—and resubmit it using the very same AUS.

When something like this occurs, the loan officer tells the veteran, "Sorry, I can't get you approved for a $210,000 loan, but I can get you approved for a $200,000 loan." With that information, the veteran can either renegotiate the sales price of the home picked out, look for a home in the $200,000 price range, or find some money somewhere to put down.

VA loans can still be approved the "old-fashioned" way, which means being approved literally by a person . . . the underwriter. Sometimes a loan doesn't get an AUS approval, but that doesn't mean the loan isn't VA eligible. It simply means there are some special circumstances that prohibit the automated approval.

Most often these circumstances involve credit issues pertaining to bankruptcies. If your loan doesn't get the AUS approval, your loan officer will tell you. Not to worry here, though, because your loan is merely approved under a different method.

An AUS simply takes the data given to it and spits out an approval with a list of items the veteran must provide. The approval might read as follows:

This loan is approved if documented with the following items:

_____ Two most recent paycheck stubs covering the most recent thirty-day period substantiating $5,000 per month gross income

_____ Three months' most recent bank statements showing $10,000 in deposit funds

_____ An appraisal showing appraised value of $300,000

_____ Homeowners insurance policy covering $300,000

And so on. If you furnish whatever the AUS asks for, as long as it is provided with the original loan application, the loan can be approved without much human intervention.

When a Loan Is Underwritten Manually

Sometimes VA loans don't get an approval using an AUS. In this case the file must be underwritten manually. This time, the underwriter goes down a list, item by item, asking for various pieces of documentation. Typically, you'll be asked for more pieces of documentation, and that's simply because the human underwriter must ask for and include everything in the loan package that might be required to cover a VA approval, even if it may not be needed directly.

For example, let's say the borrower puts down that she has three accounts at her bank totaling $25,000. But because she's getting a VA loan with no money down and reduced closing fees, she might only need $3,000 in order to close the loan. But because the three accounts were listed on the borrower's loan application, the underwriter is required to verify them.

A highly qualified veteran with sterling credit and lots of money lying around might get an AUS approval with minimum documentation required, but that same veteran would require a lot of documentation for a manual underwrite. An AUS could only ask for one paycheck stub, and that's it. But a manual underwrite would require standard documentation of the two most recent pay stubs, the two most recent W-2s, perhaps two years' worth of tax returns, and so on.

When a file is manually underwritten, it's because something occurred in the original AUS submission that didn't add up. Sometimes there is a credit issue—perhaps some collection accounts that have been paid but aren't appearing that way on the consumer's credit report. Perhaps an old bankruptcy is showing up on the credit report and is reporting errors. Most often, when an AUS can't issue an approval, it's due to credit. The file must then be underwritten manually.

At this point, the underwriter makes the determination whether the file meets VA guidelines. If a bankruptcy appears on the credit report as being less than two years old, the underwriter probably won't approve the loan, because VA lending requirements are such that a bankruptcy has to be more than two years old and the borrower has to have reestablished good credit.

If there is a mistake, however, then the underwriter will simply document the error and proceed with underwriting the file. Now a different issue arises unique to VA loans: disposable income.

Residual Income and VA Loans

Recall that the VA debt ratio stands at 41. A manual underwrite must take into consideration income that is available to the borrower after housing payments, and it must also estimate what the state and federal tax withholdings would be to calculate a "take-home pay" number. The VA calls this "residual income," and it is a relatively complex method of determining if you, in fact, have enough money each month to not only pay your bills but to also take care of daily necessities.

Why is this important? Sometimes debt ratios alone don't tell the whole story of someone's ability to repay a debt. If 41 percent of someone's gross monthly pay is covering the house payment and monthly bills appearing on that someone's credit report, that means 59 percent of someone's gross monthly pay is also available for everything else. But there's a little trick here, and it's based on income.

For instance, 41 percent of $3,000 is $1,230. A borrower's gross monthly allowable debts need to be at or near this number. That leaves $1,770 available for everything else. Everything else, first of all, means federal and state taxes. It also means perhaps supporting other members of the household. If the borrower has three kids, then after subtracting federal and state withholdings, the residual income drops to about $1,000.

Out of this number comes the phone bill, the electricity bill, food, gasoline and car maintenance, health and automobile insurance, braces for the kids, pizza a few times a month, and maybe even a movie every now and then.

Can you see how that $1,000 is eaten up?

Now take a veteran with higher income, say, $10,000 per month. Now, 41 percent of $10,000 is $4,100, leaving a gross residual income number of $5,900. Take out some taxes and the net so far is around $3,000. That $3,000 is a lot more than $1,000.

Now those braces or trips to the movies don't seem so significant because the higher wage earner, while still meeting the 41 percent ratio guideline, has more residual income each month to pay other obligations, save for emergencies, and so on.

As long as your residual income is at or above VA requirements for a manual underwrite, you'll go to the next step of approval. Because there are differences in cost of living and wages in various parts of the country, the VA has divided up the country into four regions. Figure 3–1 and Figure 3–2 are charts used to calculate residuals.

Figure 3–1. Residual income table by region, for loan amounts to $79,999 and below.

Family Size	Northeast	Midwest	South	West
1	$390	$382	$382	$425
2	$654	$641	$641	$713
3	$788	$772	$772	$859
4	$888	$868	$868	$967
5	$921	$902	$902	$1004

For 5+ family members, add $75 for each additional member, up to a family of 7.

Figure 3–2. Residual income table by region, for loan amounts to $80,000 and above.

Family Size	Northeast	Midwest	South	West
1	$450	$441	$441	$491
2	$755	$738	$738	$832
3	$909	$889	$889	$990
4	$1025	$1003	$1003	$1117
5	$1062	$1039	$1039	$1158

For 5+ family members, add $80 for each additional member, up to a family of 7.

Next, add up your house payment, property taxes, and homeowners insurance, along with other bills such as car payments, credit card obligations, or student loan payments.

If your principal and interest payment is $1,000, your taxes are $150 per month, and property insurance is $75 per month, that gives you a $1,225 monthly total. Add a car payment of $300 and a student loan payment of $50 and your total debt for the purposes of calculating residual income is $1,575.

Next, subtract your state and federal withholdings from your gross monthly income. This number is most easily found on one of your recent pay stubs. If your gross income is $4,000, approximate with-holdings for federal taxes and state taxes might be $800 per month.

Add $800 to the $1,575 debt payment and subtract that number from your gross income of $4,000:

$$\$4,000 - \$2,375 = \$1,625$$

Next, add up the number of dependents in your household and look up the residual income requirement. If your number is above the requirement, your residual income is good to go for a VA loan.

For example, if you have one dependent in your household, live in the Midwest, and your loan amount is $90,000, your minimum residual would be $738. With three people in your household, the minimum would be $889. The more family members in your household, the more the residual income requirement will change.

Calculating Your Income

Debt ratios are a result of your debt divided by your income. But your income must be calculated properly in order to arrive at the correct ratio. One key component of wages is that you must be employed full-time, with special consideration given to part-time income only if there are other full-time wages being counted elsewhere.

Income is typically divided into three basic areas:

- Hourly Wages
- Monthly Wages
- Self-Employment Income

Hourly wages are wages paid by the hour. If you get paid $10.00 per hour and work forty hours per week, then you make $400 a week. A common mistake rookie loan officers can make is to inadvertently neglect to give hourly workers enough qualifying income.

So, $400 per week times four weeks per month is $1,600 per month, right? No. Actually, there are closer to 4.25 weeks in a month. On occasion, a loan officer, while prequalifying you to buy a house, will mistakenly calculate your income using only four weeks per month, when in fact your income would be higher if calculated correctly.

The loan officer instead should multiply your weekly earnings by fifty-two, or fifty-two weeks per year, then divide that number by twelve. Debt ratios are figured using monthly income, not hourly or weekly income.

In this example, $400 per week times fifty-two weeks per year equals $20,800. Now divide that number by twelve months and the answer is $1,733 per month—not the lower $1,600 amount. If there is overtime on this particular job—say, time and a half for anything above forty hours—then that overtime amount can also be used under particular circumstances.

The employer who works an employee overtime must be able to establish that any overtime given to an employee is not of a seasonal nature or only a stopgap instance because there is a temporary labor shortage.

For example, if John makes $20 per hour and is working full-time, that works out to $3,466 per month. But if John works an additional ten hours of overtime each week, that would add another $300 weekly, or another $1,300 per month, to the borrower's qualifying income.

That's significant. Using the VA ratio of 41, that means the borrower could carry 41 percent of $4,766, or $1,954 in debt.

But what if John only began working overtime last month, when the company had an unexpected order that needed to be filled? What if John's expected $1,300 in additional monthly earnings was only supposed to last for only three or four months?

Then the lender won't be able to use that additional overtime. The income guidelines for VA loans require a history of overtime, usually documented by previous years' income tax returns and a letter from the employer suggesting that the additional ten hours per week would be continuous and be available to John for as long as he wanted.

If overtime income has a history and is likely to continue, the lender will indeed use the additional $1,300. If not, then John is forced to be qualified at the lower amount.

Another common pay method is monthly or twice monthly paychecks, such as getting paid on the first and the fifteenth of the month. This is the easiest to calculate; it's simply listed on the pay stub and the lender will use the amount from the check. If the pay period from the first to the fifteenth pays $3,000 per month, then gross monthly income is twice that, or $6,000 per month.

Self-Employed Borrowers

When income is derived from a business owned by the borrower, then there's a whole new method of calculating income: tax returns.

Hourly employees or standard wage earners are rarely asked to provide income tax returns when applying for a mortgage. Only when or if additional income or expenses are noted or discovered by the lender are tax returns asked of the hourly wage earner.

For example, let's say an hourly employee states on his application that he receives child support or alimony payments. There is a section on the Form 1003 that asks about "other income" in the Income part of the loan application. There's also a little space on the application that asks how much the borrower receives in child support or alimony each month.

When an underwriter sees there is "other income" on an application, typically the underwriter will ask for tax returns. Why? To verify how much is actually being paid. Each month. Or perhaps a divorce decree is required to determine how much a borrower pays or receives in support.

For the self-employed, however, tax returns are a requirement. There is no other way to verify income other than what is reported to the IRS via these returns. Sure, the self-employed borrower may have paycheck stubs or W-2s from his own company, but that doesn't go far enough for third-party verification status.

Filed and signed tax returns are required. There is a big difference in gross and net income for a business.

For instance, a borrower gets her income from a dog grooming business and takes in about $300,000 per year. The borrower puts $300,000 on the 1003, but will the lender use that $300,000 per year figure? No. The underwriter will review tax returns to look at other items . . . primarily the expenses necessary to run the business.

Self-employed borrowers can come in various legal forms, but perhaps the most common is the sole proprietor. In this case, the borrower will file an IRS Schedule C, which lists all of the borrower's income and subtracts expenses to get a net income amount.

It's the net income the IRS taxes, not the gross income.

Now let's get back to the dog groomer. She has additional fees, with perhaps the biggest expense going to employees who help groom the dogs. There are two people who wash the dogs, at $50,000 per year total. There are two people that cut and clip the dogs at $50,000 per year total.

So far, we've added $100,000 in expenses. The self-employed borrower has reduced her gross income to $200,000. Now comes soap. Lots of it. And flea and tick powder. And cute little bows and nail clippers. And vacuum cleaners for picking up all the dog hair.

Next we'll deduct insurance, property rental, and other expenses. At this stage, we've added up another $100,000 in annual business expenses. Our annual income is now $100,000, not $300,000.

The underwriter would never know exactly how much to use to calculate the debt ratio without seeing tax returns. Someone with a paycheck stub who is not self-employed has third-party verification of income . . . pay stubs from somebody else. The self-employed borrower doesn't have that, so the third-party verification comes from copies of filed tax returns.

In addition, the VA lender not only wants to see that the borrower can make money at her business, but also that she has a track record running a business. Besides simply grooming and walking dogs, the borrower must also know how to pay bills, handle employees, and keep sufficient supplies on hand to run the business. Every month. Every day.

That's why self-employed borrowers need to show that, at minimum, they've been self-employed for two years before applying for a VA loan. Lenders want to see a consistent pattern, and two years is that pattern.

What if the pattern is not consistent? What if a borrower has two years of experience but the two years are wildly different in income?

First, the underwriter will average the income from the previous two years filed. If one year she grooms enough dogs to make $100,000 and the next year she makes $150,000, the lender won't use the $150,000 amount but instead will add $100,000 from year one and $150,000 from year two and average them together.

Instead of $150,000 per year, or $12,500 per month, it works out to $125,000 per year, or about $10,500 per month. That's a 16 percent reduction in income. Not a big drop, but a change nonetheless.

In this example, the income increased from one year to the next. If the opposite occurred—say, the income went from $150,000 to $100,000, which is a 33 percent drop—the underwriter will be concerned.

Why did income drop so much? Is this a trend? Is she mismanaging the business? Is there competition? If income drops another 30 percent, that would reduce her income to $70,000 per year, less than half of what was recorded just two years ago.

In this instance, not only will the underwriter want to know why the income went down so much so quickly, he may in fact decline the loan. Averaging doesn't help when income drops significantly. What is significant? There are no rules, but anything beyond a 15 percent drop in net income will cause an underwriter to raise his eyebrow.

In this case, if there was a 30 percent drop in income and the business was brand-new, this could be an issue. If, however, the business has been around for several years, a temporary drop in income, even 30 percent, wouldn't harm the approval. Especially if there are other factors that would be evident to an underwriter. For instance, a person who sells winter coats for a living might happen to lose business in the middle of a weird hot spell. That would be an example of nothing more than an off business cycle.

Commissions

People who receive more than 25 percent of their income from commissions may not think they're self-employed, but their situation is actually similar to the self-employed borrower.

Commissions are monies paid to someone as a percentage of sales made. If a commissioned salesman sells chocolate bars at $2.00 each and gets 20 percent of each sale made, his commission is forty cents. If that chocolate salesman sells 10,000 candy bars per month at $2.00

each, then that's $20,000 total, and his commission would be 20 percent of that, or $4,000.

VA loans ask that commission sales have a minimum two-year history, just like the requirement for the self-employed borrower. Even though the salesman works for the candy factory, his pay structure is very similar to the business owner who actually makes the candy bars.

A VA lender will also ask for tax returns when someone has commissioned income above 25 percent of his or her gross income. If the candy guy makes $20,000 per month and his commission is only $4,000, then his commission is less than 25 percent of his income. That means no tax returns are required. If, however, he makes $8,000 per month and his commission is $5,000, then his commission exceeds 25 percent of his gross income.

Lenders might also recognize that the salesman might take his candy clients out for golf. Or buy them lunch. Or deduct mileage on his car. Or have other business-related expenses. And typically a letter from his employer is required, stating whether the employer reimburses job-related expenses.

Can someone who is paid a monthly wage also receive income from self-employment? Sure she can.

I did a loan for a woman who worked full-time for a nonprofit organization but also made another $6,000 per year from her home-based business. She needed to include the extra income to qualify for her home. Her debt ratio without the additional income hovered near 50, which is far too high for most VA loans.

She had reported her extra income on her tax returns and had a record of it from the previous two years. I was able to use that income because there was a two-year history and it was verified by a third party—the IRS.

Unfortunately, there are countless other people who have additional income that simply cannot be used. If that nice lady had additional home-based income that she didn't report because she didn't think it was enough income to worry about, then she wouldn't have gotten the home she wanted.

If you report it, you can use it. If you don't, well, you may have to worry about the IRS, and you definitely can't use it.

Bonuses

Other income that can be used on the loan application in order to qualify is from bonuses received. Bonuses can be issued at any time, but usually they're paid upon certain job performance, often to salepeople or those who reach certain goals or quotas at their jobs.

Income from bonuses is treated like other self-employed or commissioned income . . . it is averaged, verified to have a history, and determined it if is likely to continue.

Rental income can be used as additional income. If you own property and receive income from it, VA lenders will use that income as long as it's evident on the tax returns.

Dividend and interest income? Again, if there's a history, the source of funds can be identified, and the income is likely to continue, then the interest or dividend income can be used to determine debt ratios.

Compensating Factors and VA Loans

What happens, though, if your ratios are above the 41 percent guideline? What happens if your residual income requirement is t-h-i-s close? Then still another manual underwriting situation comes into play.

The VA allows for extenuating circumstances to be used when an underwriter thinks the veteran should be approved for a VA loan yet is not meeting a guideline. These extenuating circumstances are called "compensating factors."

Compensating factors are positive indicators in the file that can offset a negative one. For instance, if the debt ratio on a borrower is 43 and not 41, the underwriter will look for something that indicates the "likelihood of increased earnings." For example, if the applicant has just graduated from school with a new degree and is just entering the civilian workforce, an underwriter could physically notate the file stating, "Borrower is allowed expanded debt ratios due to likelihood of increased earnings in the near future. She has just received her law degree and her earnings should only continue to rise." In this instance, the underwriter might approve a VA loan that had a debt ratio above the required 41 guideline.

How much higher than 41 can an underwriter go? That's purely a judgment call from the underwriter's standpoint. There isn't anything that says "you can't go above 48," or some similar edict. At least from the perspective of the VA's guidelines.

Lenders may have internal guidelines that they may require, but underwriters do have latitude.

Other compensating factors might be the borrower's length of time in his current job, high residual income, or lots of money in the bank. Whatever the compensating factor is, the underwriter must come to the conclusion that the loan's not going to go into default.

Remember, all this is only necessary when a manual underwrite is required. If the loan is approved through an AUS, then residual income calculations, debt ratios, and compensating factors simply do not apply.

The underwriter will also look at how much the borrower is entitled to borrow.

On your Certificate of Eligibility, there is an amount listed as your available home loan entitlement from the VA. This is the amount the VA will guarantee your lender should you default. Lenders will then multiply your available entitlement by four to get the maximum loan amount the lender will make.

Let's look at entitlements in more depth. The VA has had archaic methods of entitlement calculations, and for a long time that entitlement amount was $10,000. In this case, a lender would issue a zero-money-down VA loan equal to four times that amount, or $40,000. The maximum loan would be $40,000.

If you can think of the VA entitlement as a "down payment" on behalf of the veteran to the VA lender, then you can understand how this works. The VA doesn't actually pay the guaranty to the lender, but the lender has a little more breathing room when making a zero down loan, knowing that there is a guaranteed amount given to the lender should the loan go bad.

As years went by, the VA gradually increased these entitlement amounts. This means that for older veterans who may have only had a $10,000 entitlement when they were discharged, over the years that amount has gone up. A lot. But because there didn't appear to be any rhyme or reason to the annual or occasional increases in entitlements, they were confusing to most veterans. The VA wanted to clear up that confusion and compete better with conventional loans, so it made a basic change.

The guaranty amount would be equal to one-quarter of the conventional loan limits. In this instance the conventional loan limit would be $417,000. In "high cost" states such as Alaska and Hawaii, this VA loan limit increases still more to $625,000, or an increase of about 50 percent over the rest of the nation's limit.

Let's say, then, that a long time ago you used your $10,000 available eligibility to buy a home and now the guaranty is at $104,250. What could you do? You can use the remaining eligibility left to buy another property by subtracting the $10,000 already used from your available $104,250 and you're left with $94,250. This special feature is available one time only.

Four times $94,250 is $377,000. Do you want to borrow more? You can reuse your entitlement to purchase another home *one time only* if you still own the previous property and the previous VA loan is paid in full. Remember that a VA loan can't be used to buy investment properties, but it can be used to buy another home that you intend to live in. The eligibility can be restored to you.

If the home you first bought has been sold to someone else, the new owner did not assume your VA loan, or the old loan on the house has been refinanced into another mortgage, then you have your eligibility restored completely. If you want the maximum loan amount, your eligibility must be fully restored. If it's not and you've used part of your eligibility to buy a home in the past and you still own the old property, you'll only be able to use your remaining eligibility one time.

VA loans used to be issued under a "nonqualifying assumption" status. That's a lot of words that simply mean someone could take over your old VA loan and release you from the debt, and the buyer wouldn't need to qualify from an income or credit standpoint.

For many years, people with credit or income challenges would look for someone who had a VA loan. They would then offer to take over the mortgage. Often, if the veteran was having a hard time making the mortgage payment, he needed someone to buy the home or else he'd lose it entirely, so he would sell. This helped the veteran get out of a difficult situation and helped someone else get into a home.

After several years, it became evident that this practice may not have been the most prudent thing for the VA to allow. Yes, veterans got out from under mortgages they could no longer afford, and someone else took over the payments, along with any other equity in the property, but the default rates on those nonqualifying assumptions were significantly higher than the rest of the industry. The VA was getting creamed with defaulting VA loans.

The VA then canceled the nonqualifying nature of VA loans in 1988, making buyers who wanted to assume a VA loan qualify all over again. If someone assumed your VA loan, your entitlement was stuck. The only way to restore your VA entitlement would be if the original loan was replaced by yet another buyer using his own financing or refinancing your old VA loan into a non-VA loan.

In these instances, your eligibility is completely restored. If not, no restoration will be granted and you'll only have available what is left from your original entitlement.

Again, just because a lender may lend up to $417,000 on a VA loan doesn't mean you'll get one; you still have to qualify from a credit and debt-ratio standpoint.

Can a co-borrower who is neither your spouse nor VA-eligible be on a VA loan with you? Yes, but lenders won't allow for a zero-money-down loan for the ineligible co-borrower. In most instances, the lender will either decline to issue a VA loan or he'll ask for some down payment, typically 5 percent from the co-borrower. Non-VA-eligible co-borrowers make it a non-VA loan.

On the other hand, can you combine two people with VA eligibility and increase their maximum VA loan limit? Sort of. You can combine each entitlement, but the loan amount still won't be higher than the current guideline. You can't get an $834,000 VA loan ($417,000 times two) for example. But one person may have a maximum loan amount of $100,000 and the other qualified veteran could also have $100,000 available, resulting in a $200,000 VA loan. Understand that such instances rarely happen, but it's possible. Normally a veteran would sell her current home, retire the VA-guaranteed note to restore her eligibility, and use her full entitlement to buy a new home.

Because there are such things as remaining eligibilities, if the veteran previously used her VA entitlement to buy a home, the home is free and clear and the veteran still owns that home. It could happen. Not often, but it could.

There are also unfortunate times when a married couple gets divorced and the home they bought was purchased with a VA loan. Depending on the settlement, a veteran might end up having to pay the mortgage on a house he doesn't live in, and at the same time he's unable to buy a new home because the entitlement is tied up in the first house. In order to restore that VA eligibility, the home loan must be refinanced into another loan completely, or sold, retiring the note.

Entitlements belong to the veteran or an otherwise qualified VA borrower.

But with all that, how do you really know what you're qualified for? First, we need to understand the levels of approval.

Grades of Approval

There are three basic grades of "approval." I know this sounds a little weird—you're thinking, either you're approved or you're not—but there are in fact three degrees and they are:

- Prequalified
- Preapproved (or approved with conditions)
- Loan Commitment

Prequalification

You may have heard the term *prequalifed* before. If not, it's a term that means that the consumer has had a conversation with a loan officer and that loan officer has determined that, according to standard VA guidelines, the consumer would probably be approved for a VA loan.

VA prequalifications are typically nothing more than a conversation between a VA-qualified borrower and a loan officer. Yes, the loan officer determined that, based on the conversation with the borrower, debt ratios were below 41 and the credit was good.

Prequalifications carry little, if any, third-party verification. It's simply a couple of people talking.

"How much money do you make?" asks the loan officer.

"About $45,000 per year," says the active duty soldier.

"Okay, how's your credit?" asks the loan officer.

"Excellent."

"Good. Based upon our conversation, you are prequalified for $XXX,XXX. Congratulations, I'll send your prequalification letter now," says the loan officer.

What has just happened is that the loan officer is sending, on letterhead, a prequalification letter that says the soldier is prequalified to borrow up to a specific amount.

Unfortunately, Realtors aren't accepting such letters today. Prequalification letters, although commonplace just a few years ago, have been determined (rightfully so, I might add) to be worthless.

Prequalification letters are nothing more than a scenario where two people have talked about a loan. Your Realtor will need something more—at minimum, a preapproval letter.

Preapproval

A preapproval takes verification a level higher . . . to third-party verification. A preapproval means the applicant's credit report was reviewed and his assets and employment were verified by reviewing bank statements and paycheck stubs, W-2s, and letters from his employer.

An alternative to the preapproval, and one now most widely used, is the *conditional approval*.

A conditional approval is typically the result of an AUS decision, although it doesn't have to be. This approval level demonstrates that the borrower is creditworthy (because the credit report was pulled during the AUS submission) and that the veteran can provide third-party documentation to prove his claims on the original loan application, such as "I make this much money" or "I have this much money" and other claims.

The most common method of obtaining a conditional approval is the AUS. And that usually occurs when you apply online. The lender doesn't have your documentation of income and employment, yet instead relies on your information being verifiable at a later date.

When an AUS isn't used to get a conditional approval, the loan file is usually documented with the basic information, such as recent pay stubs, recent bank statements, and other documents that back up the claims on the application. However, this is a lot of work, not just for the consumer but for the lender as well. It involves collecting all the documentation up front, then submitting it to an underwriter for a manual underwrite. If your loan officer goes this route at the very beginning, it's likely the loan officer is a rookie. Most all VA conditional approvals are automated, so up-front documentation isn't needed.

Commitment Letter

Finally, the highest level of loan approval is the commitment letter. The commitment letter is an official piece of paper from the lender that says, "Okay, we're done here . . . go find a house and we'll give you a mortgage on it."

Commitment letters are typically legal documents, and Realtors love them. There is no "he's approved if we can verify that he makes $200,000 per year" or some other such unverified claim.

A commitment letter also stipulates that if anything changes from when the original letter was issued, then the commitment letter is no good. If the veteran makes $5,000 per month then later gets demoted or changes jobs and only makes $4,000, then the deal is off. Or perhaps more debt is taken on during the home-searching process, increasing ratios past the 41 guideline. There are any number of other loan details that could kill a commitment.

If, however, you get your commitment letter and keep your profile exactly as it was when originally submitted, or make it better, then this gives you the highest level of confidence when making an offer to a seller. It also gives the seller of the property the same level of confidence that you've gone through everything necessary to be approved and there will be no problems, at least from the borrower's perspective.

But how do you get such a commitment or a conditional approval for that matter if you don't have a property picked out? An AUS typically needs a property address for the system to work.

In this case, your loan officer might enter a potential address. If you're going shopping, have you seen a property you might want to buy? Use that address. Or perhaps your loan officer will input a property address on his own to make the system work.

Once your information gets placed into the system and you have your conditional approval or commitment letter in hand, the wheels begin to turn. The approval is the very first part of your journey. You don't want to shop for a new home without full confidence you can qualify for a mortgage. Not knowing makes it a lot less fun.

CHAPTER 4

Finding Your VA Team

You're now at a critical step. All the homework you've done is getting ready to be put to the test. You now need to determine who will be your VA lender and who will be your Realtor.

First, though, do you even need a Realtor?

With the advent of the Internet, real estate listings can be found at the click of a mouse. Just type in a town you want to live in, or maybe a zip code, enter in your price range, and magically homes for sale that meet your criteria pop up on your screen. No need for a Realtor to do that, right? Sure. Not for that, anyway.

A common misunderstanding is that Realtors cost the buyers money. That somehow it costs you, the veteran or active duty soldier, pocket change to enlist the services of a qualified Realtor. Not true. Okay, there are certain parts of the country where a seller listing a property won't pay another Realtor for bringing a buyer to him, but that's the exception and not the rule. If there's any doubt, I'd simply pick up the phone, call a real estate company, and ask what it costs to use one of its Realtors to find a home. The answer in almost every case will be "nothing."

Realtors buy and sell homes every single day. That's their job. The "listing" Realtor is the person who is selling the home on behalf of the owner of the property and who puts the property on a list. This list is usually the Multiple Listing Service, or MLS. The "selling" Realtor is the person who brings a buyer to the table. Sometimes the selling Realtor is also called the "buyer's agent." I know, it's confusing.

If you don't use a Realtor to help you find a home and instead you find one on your own that is listed by a Realtor, that listing agent represents the seller of the property and not you.

The MLS is a central database of homes that local Realtors sub-scribe to. A Realtor has to be a member of the MLS in order to list houses and to have access to property information that the everyday consumer can't get. When you log on to a Realtor's website and see homes listed, or if you go to www.Realtor.com, those homes are being pulled from the MLS database for you to review.

When a Realtor agrees to sell a home for a seller, there is a com-mission involved. Commission rates can vary depending on what the listing agent and the seller agree upon. The listing Realtor may agree to a 5 percent commission upon sale. If the home is listed for $200,000, then the commission would be 5 percent of $200,000, or $10,000.

The listing agent may also advertise on the MLS that selling agents will be compensated, typically by splitting the commission from the seller fifty-fifty. In this example, the listing agent would then receive $5,000 and the buyer's agent would get $5,000.

So why would you need a Realtor? For the very reason that Realtors buy and sell homes every day and you do not. Your Realtor will guide you through the buying process, help arrange for inspections, help negotiate your contract, and assist you in making an offer on the prop-erty. A Realtor who is on your side is paid to represent you by receiving a split of the commission upon sale. There is simply no reason not to use a Realtor when buying a house. It costs you nothing and you're taking advantage of that Realtor's years of experience in real estate and in negotiations.

Sometimes, when you see a house you like and you go visit it at an open house, for instance, you may meet the listing Realtor. Or you're driving around the neighborhood and write down the name and number of the Realtor listed on the "for sale" sign in the front yard. Or maybe you see a listing on the Internet and give the agent a call. At this point, the listing agent probably won't pay your Realtor any commission at all. You won't get the advantage of using a Realtor without charge because your Realtor was not the "procuring cause."

Procuring cause is a real estate term referring to the party responsible for bringing a buyer to the seller. Was it the buyer's agent? Not if you found the house on your own. Did you call because you saw the listing agent's phone number on the for-sale sign? Again, you're out of luck with a buyer's agent. That is, unless you pay for one yourself.

When you call a Realtor on your own, the first question you are likely to be asked is, "Are you working with another Realtor?" And if you are, the next question will be something like, "Did she find this house for you?" If you're not working with an agent, then the Realtor might ask if you'd like to be his client, so he can help find you a home.

If you want to buy the house the listing agent is selling, then the first thing to understand is that the listing agent cannot be your agent. In other words, he won't be advising you or representing your interests. He can't advise you during the process because he's legally obligated to the seller. Besides, you don't want to negotiate with anyone whose first loyalty goes to someone you're trying to get the best deal from.

If you decide you don't want that house, then the Realtor will ask you if you'd like to have her be your Realtor and help you find a home. That's how Realtors get paid, by buying and selling houses, so if they don't ask to represent you, then they're probably not very good Realtors.

When you do your own surfing on the Internet or drive around and see a house you like that your Realtor hasn't sent to you, then stop what you're doing and call your Realtor first.

"Joe Realtor, this is David. There's a house I found that I'm interested in. It's at 123 Main Street and the listing agent is Sally Realtor." At this point, your Realtor calls the other Realtor and says, "I have someone that might be interested in your property."

Then the ball begins to roll.

Let's take a moment, though, to examine when such an occurrence would actually happen. If your Realtor is paid to find you houses, why do you have to find your own house and have your Realtor simply make an offer on your behalf?

This won't happen very often, or at the very least, it shouldn't happen at all. Your Realtor is supposed to continuously search for homes on your behalf. In fact, most MLS tools have features built in that alert the Realtor when a property comes up that meets your requirements. For instance, you know you want a home in the $350,000 range. You need four bedrooms and you want to be in a particular school district. Your Realtor can plug in these parameters in the automatic search tool embedded in the MLS. As a property is listed in the MLS, your Realtor gets notified.

Some MLS applications will alert the Realtor immediately upon being listed, or once a day, or once a week, and so forth. The Realtor merely inputs your requests and waits for a property that meets your specifications.

Sometimes, though, you find the house instead. I know, because it happened to me.

My wife and I had been searching for a home that suited us for nearly six months. Because we had three small children, we wanted to live in a particular school district, and we knew what we were qualified for.

We did find a few homes that we wanted, but for one reason or another the offers were never accepted. Once, the house didn't pass the inspection according to our standards, and a couple of other times we were simply outbid.

One day, my wife was surfing the Internet and saw a house that had just listed that day. It met all of our requirements. She called me on the phone and said to hurry down and look at this house she had found. I told her to call our Realtor first.

Anyone can look for houses. Homes are listed on the Internet and in the newspapers, but finding a home isn't exclusively what a Realtor is for. Realtors look out for you. They help negotiate contracts. They keep you out of hot water and warn you when things are looking bad.

My Realtor and I met at the house, walked through it, and after just a few minutes we wrote up an offer. The offer was accepted the next day and we were the new happy owners. But there were some things that needed to be negotiated, such as repairs we wanted done and price adjustments for various flaws we found during the course of the inspection. My Realtor negotiated these things for me based on his knowledge of what certain repairs would cost in relation to the concessions being made by the seller.

We were in an ultrahot real estate market, so sellers could be choosy. I am convinced that without my Realtor negotiating on my behalf, I would not have gotten that home, which I still own today. And it cost me nothing.

Finding a Realtor

My advice is simple: Use a Realtor.

But, in addition to that, use a Realtor who understands the VA lending process. Otherwise, you could find a Realtor who may try and talk you out of using a VA loan.

For years upon years, VA loans simply took too long, were complicated, and had pitfalls that conventional or other government loans did not have. One of these snags is that VA loans can cost the sellers more money. That's right, the sellers. One of the advantages of VA loans for the veteran can also be a disadvantage for the seller.

Veterans are limited to only certain closing costs, sometimes called "nonallowables." Veterans can pay, during the course of a VA loan, an appraisal, title charges, credit reporting fees, and other limits. Whatever is not covered has to be paid by someone else, most usually the seller of the property, although sometimes the VA lender will pay them on behalf of the veteran out of the proceeds of the loan.

As a result, when a Realtor makes an offer on a house and the listing agent sees that it involves a VA loan, one of the first reactions often is, "We don't want to pay any of the VA closing costs," which ends up hurting the offer. Realtors who do not understand how VA loans actually work might decline an offer due to these fees. (We'll discuss closing costs in more detail in Chapter 6.)

Another reason Realtors might not like VA loans is that they take too long to process. Or more properly, in the past they took too long to process.

Ordering an appraisal, called the Notice of Value (NOV), for instance, used to take weeks because the appraisal order went from the lender directly to the Department of Veterans Affairs, which then found an appraiser in the area where the house was being sold. The appraiser received the appraisal order, performed the appraisal, and then instead of delivering the appraisal to the VA lender, it went to the VA. The VA then forwarded the appraisal to the lender. The loan couldn't go anywhere until the file was documented, and VA appraisals simply took too long.

Other VA forms also had to be mailed, completed, and certified. Before the Automated Certificate of Eligibility, or ACE, everything had to be mailed. If something got lost, then you had to do it all over again. If a seller was selling her house and she also wanted to buy another house, she couldn't buy the new house until she sold hers. If the VA loan took sixty days to get processed, then her offer on her new house was also being delayed. The sellers of her new house might also have been looking at moving or buying another home and they, too, were delayed.

Delays in VA loans and nonallowable closing costs used to make some Realtors shy away from doing deals involving VA loans. But nowadays, nothing could be further from the truth. Lenders can approve VA loans in minutes, order appraisals directly, and work with VA loans under a highly automated process.

The problem is that many Realtors still don't know this. Okay, Realtors who specialize or have current experience in VA lending will almost always either advertise that fact or let you know when you're interviewing potential Realtors. But those who haven't been in the business very long or have limited experience in VA lending might try to steer you in other directions.

You're at an advantage if you live in an area where there are veterans all around. Maybe you live in a Navy town where plenty of active duty service personnel, guardsmen, and veterans live. That market dictates VA-savvy Realtors.

How do you find a good and VA-savvy Realtor in a market with lots of VA-qualified people? First off, in such an environment, most Realtors have closed VA loans and know how to work with them. A Realtor's website will usually list the areas of expertise, including VA purchases.

Who are the best Realtors in town? The ones with the most experience who have been to their fair share of closings. That's not to say that a rookie Realtor isn't any good. Far from it. There are certainly many qualified rookie Realtors.

It's simply my opinion that when buying a house, which is something you'll do only a few times in your entire life, you need every absolute advantage you can get for your particular transaction. And getting an experienced Realtor is one of those advantages.

The best Realtors in town are also the ones with most of the listings. If you're looking at a Realtor's website and see several different Realtors on the site, take a look at the ones with the most houses for sale. These are the listing agents who are the most experienced.

But, you're wondering, if you call one of these listing agents up and ask about one of their listings, aren't you defeating your purpose of getting a Realtor to act as your agent? Yes, so try a couple of things.

First, try to find a listing agent who may not have the most listings in his office but has some. Stay away from agents with zero listings. It's not that they're not any good right out of the gate, mind you, but remember you need to stack as many chips in your favor as possible.

When you find the top listing agent, you're probably looking at the most successful agent in that office. In this case, you may not be working with that Realtor directly but instead with her assistant. So try to find someone in the middle of both extremes. Not the very, very best but not the worst, either.

Another idea would be to find a Realtor who has plenty of listings yet doesn't have anything you're interested in. In this case, the Realtor won't be trying to sell you one of her current listings but instead will act on your behalf as a buyer's agent. This is the ideal approach—finding a strong agent who will work 100 percent on your behalf. If you're fortunate enough to find a Realtor with lots of listings who also agrees to be your buyer's agent, you've found a successful Realtor with the ability to find listings better than most.

Finding a VA-Savvy Agent in a Town Where There Are Few Veterans

What if you're in a town or part of the country where there is no standard contingent of veterans or active duty service personnel and

VA loans are rare? It's in this instance where you really need to be careful about whom you choose to act as your Realtor.

If VA loans are a rarity in your area, it's possible your Realtor will discourage you from obtaining a VA loan simply out of ignorance about current VA lending procedures. If you find an agent who closed a VA loan five years ago and it was a nightmare, you can bet that Realtor related that experience to other real estate professionals in the office or at company functions.

VA loans are different in a few ways, and anything that's different has a learning curve. What if the Realtor only interacts with veterans who want to use their VA entitlement once every five years? You can see how a Realtor might act when you say you're looking for a home and you want to use your VA eligibility.

In this case, you should choose a Realtor who has a good working relationship with an experienced lender—someone who knows how to close a VA loan. Although it's important to find a Realtor experienced in negotiating on your behalf and finding homes that meet your requirements, it's absolutely critical that you find a loan officer who knows how to work a VA loan.

If you live on or near a military base, then you can bet there are more than a few loan officers who know their way around a VA loan. If you live near Ft. Hood, Texas, home of the 4th Infantry Division, you could probably shake a tree somewhere and a few VA loan officers will fall out.

But whom do loan officers work for? They can work for banks or mortgage bankers, or they can be mortgage brokers. And most mortgage companies offer VA loans as part of their loan portfolios.

Mortgage bankers can be a division of a large bank, or they can be independent. Although some mortgage bankers are well-known, most may be people you've never heard of. Mortgage bankers approve loans themselves and use their institution's own money or credit line to make a home loan.

Another popular source of VA funds is a mortgage broker. Brokers do not make the mortgage loan, nor do they offer any other financial services such as automobile loans or checking accounts. A mortgage broker's job is to find a mortgage for his customer at competitive rates.

Before I went to work for myself, I started in the mortgage business as a mortgage broker in San Diego, California. Later in 1995, I moved to Austin, Texas, and worked for a mortgage banker. In 1998, our company was bought by a bank and I produced mortgage loans for a bank that offered not only mortgages but also credit cards, student loans, insurance, checking and savings accounts, certificates of deposit, and everything else a bank typically offers.

So where do you start? Should you start at your bank? Should you find a mortgage banker or a mortgage broker? I've worked for all three and they all have their unique advantages.

Banks. Start where you feel comfortable: at your own bank or credit union—the place where you have your checking or savings account. Call your bank or credit union, make an appointment, and visit with them. Tell them ahead of time that you've VA eligible and you want a VA loan. Banks may not always have the very best interest rates (we'll discuss VA rates in more detail in Chapter 5), but they have something no one else would have: your trust.

Face it, you keep all your money in a bank or credit union, so they know all about you, at least from a financial perspective. And it's an entity you know. There's a relationship. Banks know that because you're their customer, they have an advantage others may not have: They already handle all your finances, or at least most of them. Their interest rates are typically posted in the bank lobby or on their website. There's little room for negotiation on rates or fees, but you know you're not going to be snookered into a raw deal. The trust factor helps.

I know from experience. When I worked for a bank's mortgage department, almost every one of our mortgage customers had an account with one of our bank's different divisions. Either they had a credit card or a student loan or a savings account. Few people came to us because we had the lowest rate: We didn't. We had their confidence.

And you should also have confidence in your banking or credit union institution. If you already trust them with your money and vital information regarding who you are, where you live, how much money you make, your Social Security number, and your PIN on your ATM card . . . well, who else can you trust with your mortgage? Financially speaking, of course.

You can also get discounts on other financial services when you get your mortgage from your bank or credit union. You can get free checking or free safety deposit boxes or free cashier's checks or whatever. Banks can envelop you with everything financial and sort of "pay" you for it.

I recall that when I got a mortgage from my bank, I also got a slew of other services for free. I no longer had to pay a monthly checking account fee, I got free checks, and my ATM withdrawals were free, plus I had a safety deposit box (which I never used, by the way) and a host of other services. Individually, those items didn't add up to much, but if I had my mortgage at another institution, I'd probably lose about $100 a month if I used those services at another bank. Do you need a safety deposit box? Would you like free checks? No ATM charges? Trust me, those are charges that add up.

In fact, if your bank offered you a 6.25 percent interest rate on a $150,000 thirty-year mortgage, the monthly payment would be near $919 per month, principal and interest. If you went to another place for a mortgage and found a VA rate at 6.00 percent, your payment would be about $895 each month. But if your checking account costs you $20 per month and ATM fees cost another $20 each month, then combined with your $895 mortgage payment that adds up to $935 per month when you get your mortgage from somewhere other than your bank or credit union. You may or may not use each and every service your financial institution might offer, but hey, why not take a look at it, right?

So, the first place to look for a mortgage loan is at your bank or credit union. You may not end up there, but it's a good place to start. Keep in mind that some banks that offer loans don't intend to keep them. So if you're considering going with your bank, you should ask whether it intends on selling the loan. This information may affect your decision.

Mortgage Bankers. The next consideration is the pure mortgage banker. These companies do nothing but home loans. As such, their specialization typically results in lower rates for their customers. When I worked for a bank, my VA rates might have been higher than what a mortgage banker could provide. When I was a mortgage banker, I could most always beat a bank's VA rate.

That's why you should try a mortgage banker as well. For the lower rate. Yes, there are other considerations, such as checking account fees and so on, but you want to make sure that you're ultimately getting the best deal, so you should also look around for lower rates. Mortgage bankers have to compete only for your mortgage business and nothing else. And because they're the mortgage lender, they can get pretty skinny when they need to be. Banks don't have to; they're your bank.

Mortgage bankers also perform other mortgage-related services that keep their costs down, such as approving the loan, underwriting it, printing closing papers, managing the overhead of keeping and securing a credit line, and so on. So do banks, but they also require overhead for the other services they offer unrelated to mortgages. Think of it as an automobile oil-change shop that will change your oil for $15. Or a dealership that will change your oil for more than that but also sells cars, does mechanical work, and pays a lot of money for the huge footprint it occupies. As a mortgage banker, our office was but a few thousand square feet. A bank's office space might be a whole lot more, with a whole bunch of other people who have nothing to do with your VA loan.

Mortgage Brokers. Your next choice is a mortgage broker. A broker does nothing except compare VA rates from different VA lenders and hope to find you the best rate available. How do brokers work?

Most every mortgage company and bank you've ever heard of has a special division called "wholesale" that caters to mortgage brokers. Brokers don't make the loan; instead, they take a VA application and compare rates from other wholesale VA lenders. Mortgage lenders have these wholesale divisions within their companies because they're a profit center for them. Wholesale mortgage companies are mortgage bankers that solicit mortgage brokers, not home loan borrowers.

If you live somewhere that doesn't have any sort of military or guard presence or there aren't a lot of retired veterans in your neighborhood, then be prepared to do some homework to find a good VA loan officer.

First, ask your Realtor or search the Web specifically for a VA lender in your city. You can expect some bumps in the road, so you need someone with experience. VA lending isn't rocket science, but experience counts, especially when you're closing on your new house within thirty days.

You may find a good choice if you work directly with your bank or credit union and it has someone who specializes in VA loans. But you have to ask for their specialty. Too often loan officers can specialize in loans for first-time home buyers, Federal Housing Administration (FHA loans), conventional loans, construction loans, loans for people with bad credit, VA loans, and jumbo loans. If you think about it, there's not much "specialty" in any of that. Someone who claims to specialize in everything can simply be "competent" in those loans. A jack-of-all-trades but king of none, so to speak. No, you want someone with solid VA experience.

But don't just get one referral, get two or three. Three is probably the best, but never contact just one loan officer. Give yourself some choices, then call those loan officers and speak with them. Ask them a few questions and get to know them better. During the initial phone call, engage them in a conversation. Get them to open up a little bit, get to know them. Just chitchat for a bit and begin asking a few questions in a roundabout way to find out certain things about them, specifically, "How long have you been in the business and how many VA loans have you closed?"

If you jump right in and ask this question at the very start, you might not establish a very good relationship. You might, but you've made it a bit more difficult. Your loan officer will be your main contact when getting approved for your loan, choosing interest rates, and negotiating closing costs.

But, by gradually leading up to the question of experience, you can ask in a nice way while still getting to a very important piece of information. After all, if you were looking for an attorney to help defend yourself against a frivolous lawsuit filed by some crazy guy who thought you took his lawn mower, would you want a divorce attorney or would you want someone more experienced in civil and criminal law?

A key question you can ask to find out how literate a loan officer is with VA loans is: "Are you LAPP [pronounced *lap*] approved?"

LAPP means Lender Appraisal Processing Program, and it is a VA-only term that VA lenders and VA loan officers know about. It's simply a streamlined method of ordering appraisals. No big deal, but if you're not familiar with VA loans, you won't know what LAPP means.

This is a quick-test question. If the loan officer stammers or wants to check back with you later, find someone else.

The answer you want to hear is, "Yes, sir, we order our appraisals directly." That loan officer has passed the test. You can move on to other questions if you wish.

For example, another key question is: "Are you set up with ACE, or do you process loans manually?"

A loan officer comfortable with VA loans might answer: "We're set up with ACE, but ACE may not have all the information in it, but we always try that first."

Once you've found two VA loan officers, which do you choose? We'll get into finding the best rate in Chapter 5 and closing costs in more detail in Chapter 6, but initially, if everything between the two loan officers is essentially the same, it simply comes down to who you feel more comfortable with.

This brings up an interesting question: Should you absolutely never work with someone who has never worked a VA loan? Or even, should you work with someone who has only been in the business for a few months?

Given the choice, probably not. But if you do decide to work with someone with very little experience, it's not the end of the world. Hey, I was a rookie once. Everyone is at some stage of his or her career. If the officer is green, ask whether he's working with a more experienced broker who will help if bumps come up in the process.

It's not a requirement that you work with a VA-lending veteran; it's just that it helps. If you choose a rookie who doesn't have resources to back him up and support him, and if there's a chance something can go wrong, then, yes, find someone else. But if your rookie loan officer has someone behind her that you can count on, then certainly put her on your short list. Hey, I wouldn't be here today if no one worked with rookies, right?

Finding Help If You're on Active Duty

Now here's another twist: How do you find a good Realtor and a good VA loan officer if you're active duty and not exactly across the street from any real estate office? Maybe you're a few time zones away, say, in Misawa, Japan.

How do you interview someone? How do you find a good loan officer? A Realtor?

Although odds are that you won't make any real estate purchases while stationed overseas, it's possible you just might have to if you find a property that you simply have to have. In this case, if you begin to get the real estate bug and think that buying real estate is what you want to do, you'll need to rely on buddies or family back home. But you can first do a little homework on your own.

The best way to start searching for a home is using the Internet and logging on to Realtor.com. This is the official website for the National Association of Realtors, and it has most of the information on real estate from all the various Multiple Listing Services from around the country.

If your home is in Chicago, then you can log on to Realtor.com, type in the zip code, the city, the price range, number of bedrooms and such, and a list of properties will come up that meet your criteria.

Don't live in Chicago? Live in a smaller town? Maybe a little town like Altus, Oklahoma, home of the 97th Air Mobility Wing? You can do the very same thing. Type in where you want to live and properties will pop up on your screen that meet your specs. Not every single MLS sends listing data to Realtor.com, but most do, regardless of size.

If you start getting intrigued by a few properties and are ready to get a little more serious than just surfing the Internet, you'll need a Realtor. You'll also need someone back home who can help. Call or e-mail your buddies back home and tell them that you need a good Realtor and a VA loan officer to help. Have them follow the very same steps outlined in this chapter, and have them give you referrals.

One of the neatest things about the Internet and e-mail is that communication can take place at your leisure, so you don't have to worry about leaving voice messages on an answering machine or posting a letter. Which is what you would have to do, or otherwise call stateside when it's two o'clock in the morning your time and four in the afternoon back home. Hardly makes for proper decision making, does it?

I recall a soldier stationed overseas who was buying a home in Alabama. I lived and worked in Texas. We never spoke, we exchanged e-mails. Maybe we spoke once, or if I recall, he left a message on my voice mail, but the bulk of the communications were by e-mail. He applied online at my website, we communicated through the Internet, and his loan papers were delivered for his review as secure e-mail attachments to his home overseas. He sent me scanned copies of his pay stubs, his bank statements, his sales contract . . . everything was done via the Internet. And his brother was his power of attorney to sign all the paperwork back home in Alabama.

Power of Attorney for Active Duty Applicants

Active duty overseas can present additional financial problems, but in anticipation of being away for a while, certain things are done to make sure everything stateside is set and taken care of while the soldier's away. One of those things is to make certain any financial affairs can be taken care. Often this means someone is assigned the right to enter into contracts or sign specific documents on behalf of the soldier stationed away.

This empowerment is called a "power of attorney," or sometimes POA, for short. Most often, this POA is given to a soldier's spouse or relative. In the case of real estate, for example, a husband and wife must both sign the closing papers. A husband can't sign for his wife if she's not present; he simply can't write her name then initial it off to the side somewhere. Nor can the wife sign and leave the husband off entirely.

Active duty is one legal instance where a POA comes into force, where the POA has the same legal authority as if the individual signed the document herself. This can be of great assistance with legal papers or loan documents, because the person with the POA can sign on your behalf and no papers need to be sent, notarized, or overnighted to some remote location.

Be careful, though, when it comes to real estate loans. Most lenders have their very own special POAs written up by their attorneys that are specific to them. Sometimes, too, a real estate loan requires a real-estate-specific POA. POAs can be general or they can be specific, meaning some lenders may not accept a general POA where someone can sign for anything on someone else's behalf.

One of the things you need to uncover when finding a lender is if you need a POA for a real estate transaction, and if the lender has a specific POA that applies only to itself. You need to make this determination at the very beginning of the process, not toward the end of the loan approval.

Lenders have lawyers, and one of the things lawyers do best is to review things. And they can take a long time to do it, or at least to get around to it. It's not uncommon for loan papers to be sent to a closing department and for the lender to find out only at the end that the closing department will be utilizing a POA during the closing. Then the lender will demand that the POA be reviewed.

Well, lawyers wouldn't be lawyers if they didn't have something they didn't object to. And when they do, no closing takes place. The POA needs to be reviewed, revamped, or scrapped entirely and replaced with a new one that the lender's lawyers have already reviewed.

It's also very possible your loan officer won't know to ask whether you are going to be using a power of attorney for your closing, so you'll need to bring it up. If you're working with a mortgage broker, it's possible the broker hasn't decided which VA lender she'll send your loan to, so remember to ask later on, when your lender has been selected, so you can have its POA available for you.

Sometimes, but not often, a lender won't have a real-estate-specific POA. In this case you will simply want to review the POA you already have. If you do have a POA, you'll need to get it to the lender for its holy water to be thrown upon it.

Don't have a POA? A good place to get one is from whoever will be handling your closing. If your closing is being handled at an attorney's office, she'll have one for you, for sure. If your closing is being held at a title company, the title company can usually get one for you. Or if your closing is being held at an escrow company, most often escrow companies have relationships with title companies that can scrounge one up for you.

The most important thing about POAs is to get them early and have them reviewed by the lender or the lender's attorneys as early as possible. There are simply too many things going on in a real estate transaction, and you don't want something as simple as a POA to slow things down. And slow them down they will, if the POA hasn't been approved beforehand.

When your loan officer asks that you start gathering all your documentation such as bank statements or paycheck stubs, this is the point where you should get your POA reviewed (if you need one). Remember, your loan officer may not know enough to ask.

Do You Get the Realtor or Loan Officer First?

But which now comes first, the chicken or the egg? Or more properly, the real estate agent or the loan officer? Realtors will want you to start with them at the very beginning of the process, to help steer you in the right direction and have at their disposal their bevy of affiliates that will help you along the way. Those affiliates include lenders, and one of the first things a Realtor will ask you is, "Have you been preapproved for a mortgage or applied with a mortgage company?"

If you haven't, then that's the very first place your Realtor will send you: to a lender to get qualified for a mortgage loan.

There is also a recent push by mortgage companies to start your home-buying process with them and not with a Realtor. Their logic is "Know what you can afford to buy before you even go shopping."

Most often when you do start with a mortgage company, the loan officer will ask you if you have a Realtor. If you don't, he'll give you a list of a couple of Realtors he does business with (and exchanges referrals with) and will tell you to take your qualification letter to the Realtors he's given you.

Which is best? Quite honestly, it doesn't really matter. Your Realtor and your mortgage lender might disagree with me there. Yes, you want to be approved for the amount you can qualify for, meaning you'll be looking at the houses in your price range, but there's no real difference if you go first to a Realtor or to a lender. Either way, you'll end up at the lender's office pretty darn quick.

Besides your Realtor and your loan officer, there are a whole host of players you may or may not ever even meet or talk to. They're also on your team, and they're the ones who provide all the other pieces to your loan puzzle. It's especially important that you know who these people are and what they do, to make sure you're getting the best possible service and value from each. These other team players are your:

- Loan Processor
- Appraiser
- Inspector
- Insurance Agent
- Title Agent
- Attorney
- Surveyor
- Underwriter
- Escrow Agent or Closer
- Funder

Okay, I understand we left one important person out . . . you. You're the most important person in this process, and I'm not saying that just to make you feel good. The reason is this: If you don't buy that house, no one—I mean no one—makes any money.

Understand that if there are things you don't understand, or if too much foreign terminology is being bandied about that it makes matters too confusing, then step back, take a deep breath, and ask a question or two. You're the boss. Always remember that. That being said, your most important contact besides your Realtor and your loan officer is your loan processor.

The Loan Processor

The loan processor will in fact be the most important person in your deal after you get an accepted sales contract. Why? Your loan officer, if she's done her job right, anyway, has already taken your loan application, reviewed your credit, and reviewed rates and closing costs. But after you get an accepted offer on a house, she's out getting more loans. So you'll be handed over to the loan processor. You'll talk to this person nearly every day. Or at least communicate via e-mail daily, especially very early on in the process.

This is not to say you'll never hear from your loan officer again. You certainly will. It's just that the wheels start to move and now it's the processor's turn to take over.

The processor will talk or otherwise communicate with every other person on that list. Your loan officer won't, nor will your Realtor. But the processor will.

Appraisers will do the Notice of Value, or NOV. An attorney will provide title insurance and maybe hold your closing, and inspectors will inspect. But it's the processor's job to pull everything together and put all the documentation in one big happy loan file to present it to the underwriter, who will sign off on your loan request. (We'll look at the NOV in more detail in the next section.)

The loan processor will contact the appraiser and order the appraisal. The processor will e-mail or fax your sales contract to the appraiser and to your chosen insurance agent, who will provide an insurance policy covering your property. Your processor will order the title, make sure a survey is ordered if one is needed in your area, order closing papers, and work on loan conditions. Your processor is truly the one who "spins plates" by taking everyone's contribution to your loan closing and putting it in an understandable format.

When a loan goes to an underwriter to be signed off, it's the processor's job to make sure the file is actually ready to be submitted. A loan can't be sent to an underwriter with one pay stub when the loan requires two stubs. Or a loan can't be submitted for a final approval without an appraisal.

In fact, when your loan gets submitted to the underwriter, everything is supposed to be there. If it's not, then the loan either gets pushed aside or sent back to the processor.

There are a few rare situations when a loan can be submitted partially. That means a lender will go ahead and underwrite a mortgage loan based on certain assumptions. For instance, a loan requires two years of W-2s but you can only find one and are still looking for the other one. The processor will typically go ahead and submit your file for final approval, based on the assumption that you do in fact have that second W-2 but you just can't put your fingers on it right now. You'll need to find the missing W-2—you can't close without it—but a minor item shouldn't hold up the entire file.

NOV not completed? No title work? No credit report? Major credit and property items will cause the file to stop dead in its tracks, but minor items the borrower has or can easily get can occasionally be overlooked.

Or what if a processor does submit a loan file, but the underwriter has some questions about the file submitted? Let's say that your loan requires $3,000 in closing costs. Although the bank account statements show that you have $4,000, the underwriter notices that there was a rather large deposit in that account that is unusual. It doesn't match up with your monthly paycheck. The deposit is maybe $3,000 or so. The underwriter may go ahead and continue approving the loan but issue a "condition" on the file, stating that before any loan papers will be drawn, you must explain where the $3,000 deposit came from.

When rather large deposits appear in a borrower's account, the underwriter wants to make sure those funds belong to the borrower and weren't part of another loan somewhere, both encumbering the real estate to be purchased as well as affecting debt ratios. The underwriter will call or e-mail the processor and say something like, "I'll sign off on this loan, but first I need to get an explanation about where this $3,000 came from."

This is called a *loan condition*. Loan conditions are typical on almost every loan. Few loans go down the pike without the underwriter requesting something, such as insurance coverage or a loan disclosure form that needed to be signed. And it's your processor who requests those things from you. It's your processor who will call or e-mail you and ask for certain documentation. This is why you'll talk to her at this stage of your loan approval and not your loan officer.

Your processor will interact with most every other party in your transaction in a similar way, putting the file together while answering questions and processing the file as you go.

Did your NOV come in low? Did you buy a house for $200,000 but the value came in at $195,000? Or perhaps the title report arrived and it shows there's a lien on the property that no one had previously known about. It's your processor who reviews all your documentation to make sure it complies with the loan requirements.

The Appraiser

The appraiser is the person who creates your Notice of Value. The NOV is a new name for the Certificate of Reasonable Value, or CRV.

These terms will interchange for a while until everyone gets used to using the new acronym. When you hear someone talk about a CRV, he or she really means the NOV or appraisal.

Using the LAPP system, your appraisal is automatically ordered from a VA-approved appraiser who will complete the order. Ordering your NOV is one of the first functions a processor will perform on your file after you've received an accepted contract.

The appraiser determines the value of your new home, primarily in two basic ways: the cost approach and the market approach.

The *cost approach* is simply nothing more than adding the approximate value of your land or lot, based on similar lots in your area, then adding the material cost estimate of what it would take to duplicate your new home from scratch. So many nails, so many boards, so many personnel hours, and so on.

The most important valuation piece, however, is not the cost approach but the *market value* of your property (hence the term, Notice of Value).

A home might cost $150,000 in hammers and nails, and the lot might go for $50,000, but does that automatically make for a $200,000 home? Nope. The true value of a piece of property is the highest price the buyer is willing to pay compared with the lowest price the seller is willing to accept.

When those two variables meet, that's the market value. That's the sales price of the home. Note, when determining market value, no other external forces can be present that could skew the true value of a home.

For example, sometimes during a divorce a couple will sell below market just to get rid of the darned thing, or perhaps there was a death in the family, or perhaps the owners were going through some rough financial times and had to sell to avoid a foreclosure. If any such external influence is evident during a home sale, then true market value will be harder to determine.

In certain areas, a home that would cost $200,000 to build from scratch would also fetch a sales price much higher than that. Let's say a home was in a highly desirable public school district, or the home was in an older, established neighborhood with lots of quiet streets and parks. These are examples of external factors that add value to a home.

That's why the cost approach isn't as relevant to value as market value.

While we're on the issue of value, let me make a serious point about what can happen when the NOV comes in higher or lower than the sales price.

Rarely will an NOV not match a sales price. The NOV will take similar homes in the area that have sold in the previous twelve months and compare those sales prices with what you just offered for your new home. These comparable homes, called "comps," must be similar in size and nature and within a reasonable distance to the subject property—namely, your property.

No two properties are exactly alike, but they can be similar. An appraiser will look up the sales price of a certain comp, then make certain allowances or "adjustments" that the appraiser will use to come to a reasonable value.

These adjustments could come in the form of one home having a pool and having 300 more square feet. Or the lot could be larger, or have more trees, or it might even have a view of downtown or some other desirable landform. After these adjustments are made, the appraiser throws all that data into a pot and arrives at a calculated NOV.

But sometimes this doesn't happen. Sometimes the value comes in differently. And here's what happens when it does.

If the NOV comes in higher, then you've just got yourself a deal. At least according to the appraiser. You bought a home at $200,000 and the NOV came in at $210,000. You can't use that additional value as "equity." You don't have $10,000 suddenly available to you. If, however, you sold that home again today, it's possible you'd get $210,000.

Many new homeowners think, "Woo-hoo! I can use that extra $10,000 for my closing costs!" Wrong. This is a common misconception. That sudden, extra equity exists on "paper only" and is not available to you for your transaction.

On the other hand, if the appraisal comes in low, then there can be real problems. Lenders make loans based upon the lower of the sales price or appraised value.

If you bought a home for $200,000 and the appraisal came in at $195,000, then you no longer have a zero down loan; you have to come into the closing with that additional $5,000 because your new VA loan will be $195,000, not $200,000.

This rarely happens, but when it does, realize you've got some choices to make. Most sales contracts give you an out if the NOV comes in below the sales price.

The Inspector

Don't confuse the inspector and the appraiser. They perform different functions and are not the same.

There are two types of inspections, although one inspector can often perform both functions. There's the structural and physical inspection, and there's the pest inspection.

A structural or physical inspection involves a walk around the house to make sure the light switches and the garbage disposal work. The inspector inspects the wiring and plumbing to make sure it's up to code. She can crawl through an attic to look at your vents, your roof, and your chimney. She crawls on top of your roof to see how your shingles are doing. She runs the dishwasher to see if it works.

Home inspections seem to be popular in some parts of the country and not necessarily in others, but for the life of me I do not know why some people decide against getting an inspection.

Let's examine this issue a little closer. When people sell their homes they spend lots of time, effort, and money getting their houses in tip-top shape. Some sellers sometimes joke that because their house looks so good again, they don't want to sell! What looks good to the eye can cover up things you would never even know about if you didn't spend the $400 or so for an inspection.

One form you'll encounter when you're evaluating the purchase of a property is called the seller's disclosure form. It's a big long checklist that the seller must complete with questions like, "Does the sink work?" "Do the toilets work?" "Does the roof leak?" and so on.

Sellers can be held financially liable if they lie about the status of a known condition. But what sellers know about a property can be different from what is actually occurring in the property. A seller may not know that there is considerable condensation in the attic due to an air-conditioning vent problem, but your inspector will find that out.

Sometimes if you are buying a brand-new home or condo an inspection may not be a requirement, but I'd still recommend it. Just because a home is new doesn't mean everything is installed properly, up to code, and working properly. If you're looking at an existing property that isn't brand-new, you should definitely get an inspection. Inspections cost around $400, depending on the services rendered and what part of the country you're in, and they are well worth it. Hey, you insure your car, don't you? Ensure a clean inspection before you buy.

Often structural inspectors can also do a pest inspection, but again, it varies from state to state. Pest inspectors look for termites or other wood-destroying pests. They can look for any pest, including ants or rodents.

Some states have lenders that require termite inspections be performed. Not all states have such a requirement, but in states where termites are more prevalent, then you're likely to find a termite requirement.

If a pest inspector finds active termites or evidence of previous termite infestation (termite marks are found on wood stairs, for instance), then the lender will stop everything and require that the home be rid of termites, either by treatment or by statement from the pest inspector that termites no longer infest the property.

Even in states where termite inspections aren't required to close the loan, if an inspector notes in her report that termites have been there before, then lenders will still want assurances that their collateral is not about to be breakfast, lunch, and dinner for some unwanted insects.

The Insurance Agent

You know this person—or at least this is the person you're probably the most familiar with in the whole real estate deal. You may have automobile insurance or have spoken with some insurance person over the phone, and you know what that person does.

If something bad happens to your house, your insurance company will usually fix it. Where do you find insurance companies? Most often you'll start with the same place where you keep your auto insurance, because you can get discounts on multiple policies. One for home, one for auto, for instance.

Whatever the case, shopping for homeowners insurance should also be a shopping routine. Don't just take for granted one insurance company is the same as the next . . . they're not.

Okay, they all insure things, but they may have different rates and different discounts for different aspects of coverage. Certain insurance companies will cover certain things that others won't. Some companies may cover particular types of water damage—for example, water damage caused by an appliance leak compared to a broken water main.

Shop, shop, shop for insurance, and make sure you're comparing apples to apples. Make sure the company has been around for a while, and certainly do your due diligence because insurance coverages can vary in fee. You can get information about insurance agents from personal referrals, a current relationship, or from your Realtor.

The insurance agent will issue to your loan processor a piece of paper called the Declaration of Coverage page, or "Dec Page," which shows how much is covered and the terms if any claims are made. Most often, lenders require coverage equal to the loan amount they're issuing. If you're getting a $200,000 loan, then the lender will like to see at least that much in coverage.

But, from a personal perspective, pay attention to your agent when insurance comes into play. You may have a $200,000 loan and you're insured up to that amount, but what if the "replacement cost" is more than that? What if you have some very nice granite tiles, artwork, personal belongings, or other things that need to be covered in case of a disaster?

What a VA lender may require and what you need to insure can be two very different things. Find a good insurance agent.

Title Agent

Okay, now here's where it gets a little interesting. Title insurance is relatively unique to real estate. It's an insurance policy that guarantees that whoever is selling you his or her property has every legal right to do so, and that you will be the sole owner of that property once money changes hands.

Think about that for a moment. Say you go buy a big-screen TV from someone advertising in the newspaper. You call him up, visit his house, and turn on the set to make sure it has a good picture and all of the buttons work. (This is your physical inspection.) You can also check out the manufacturer, look up what that model of TV originally sold for, and compare it with other big screens currently for sale, both new in stores and used in the classifieds. (This would be your appraisal.) Heck, if you looked hard enough, you could even find someone to insure it, and you would certainly have it covered under a renter's or homeowner's policy. (This would be your insurance.)

But is the seller of the big screen the legal owner? Is the big screen stolen? What if you buy that television and you get a knock on the door from someone claiming that that television set was stolen and you bought it illegally and it rightfully belongs to them, so give it back?

If you had a title insurance policy on that big-screen TV, you'd tell the person at your door to take it up with the title insurance company. But you can't buy title insurance for a television, so you have to call the cops instead.

Title insurance for real estate is necessary for several reasons, but one of the main reasons is the sanctity of owning one's home. If you have an issue with a car or any automobile, someone simply comes and picks it up. Not so with a home. There are so many consumer protections when it comes to real estate that nothing can compare.

When you get a VA loan, your VA lender wants to make sure that you, and only you, own that property and no one else has a claim to it. That's what title insurance is for. And, yes, just like any other insurance policy, there are claims, most often from unrecorded interests in the property, fraud, or forgery.

It can happen more often than you think. For example, a couple buys a condo, but the husband isn't at the closing. The wife signs for him, but she doesn't have the proper authority to do so.

Later, that couple gets divorced and he leaves the country. She sells the property to someone else. A year later, the husband arrives back to the States to find out his home was sold. He goes to his old home, knocks on the door, and says, "Hi, I'm a legal owner of this home . . . please get out."

This scenario could happen in a community-property state and it would be covered under title insurance: claims of fraud, forgery, unrecorded legal claims, or anything else that can mess up a completely clean transfer of property.

There are different policies written for title insurance: There is an owner's policy that protects the owner from claims, there is a lender's policy that protects the lender, and a few variations thereof.

Title insurance is not just a recommendation; lenders won't make a loan without it. When you apply for your VA loan and you go to your closing, you will see an entry for title insurance. In fact, before a lender issues your closing papers, it will want to review the title report to make sure you will receive clean ownership.

Your title insurance is most likely going to be chosen for you as part of the terms of your sales contract. Most often, the listing agent picks out a title company. If the buyers don't want that title company (for whatever reason), then there is still room to choose, but almost all buyers have a title agency provided to them. It's not something you have to go out and get on your own.

Sometimes, homes aren't sold using a real estate agent. Sometimes the seller of a property sells the home herself. At the same time, not everyone will need to get a home loan. Perhaps someone wants to pay cash. If you ever find yourself in the situation of paying cash for a home or otherwise buying a property without outside financing, the first thing you should do is contact a title insurance company and get quotes on coverage. You need a title insurance policy whether you have a mortgage or not. It's that important.

Attorneys

Attorneys can be very influential in a real estate transaction in one part of the country, but in other parts of the country they're nowhere to be found. You might sometimes wonder why real estate sales aren't treated the very same way in each and every state.

In fact, there are no national laws that require real estate to be sold in a particular fashion or with certain procedural laws. Yes, there are discrimination laws and loan disclosure requirements, but there is no national standard.

This is because real estate is local, and real estate law is written under each state code. In some places, an attorney is required to review all closing papers; or in others not. Whatever the state regulations say, that's how the closing will take place. This means that the closing must adhere to the closing laws of whatever state the property is located in. If you live in New York and want to buy property in Florida, then the closing laws of Florida will rule.

Attorneys can vary in importance. In Texas, for instance, it's a law that attorneys must review all mortgage loan documents before they can be signed by the buyer or seller. Attorneys don't represent the buyer or seller, yet no loan can close without an attorney's review.

In such cases, attorneys aren't looking out for the interests of either party; instead, they are making claims that the loan documents conform to the law.

In Illinois, attorneys can provide a title policy, but they also hold the real estate closing. All sales contracts must first be reviewed by an attorney.

In California, real estate attorneys are not involved. You don't need a lawyer in California to close a deal. Sometimes real estate lawyers are called in to address certain buyers' rights or sellers' rights, or even to mediate a squabble, but they're not required like they are in Texas and Illinois. Find out what your state requires. A good Realtor can help you with this issue and suggest a real estate lawyer.

Surveyor

The surveyor is the person who physically measures the lot the house sits on, along with boundary lines, easements, and all permanent structures.

A surveyor doesn't inspect the home or determine its value like an appraiser. This person simply surveys things such as fence lines, sidewalks, the house, a shed, a pool . . . anything that can't be picked up and hauled away.

A survey will also show the exact property lines. If you wake up one morning and see your neighbor building a new fence but it looks like it's awfully close to your property, then you'd want to pull out your survey and check the property markings to see if, in fact, your nice neighbor is building on your property. If he is, he must tear it down and start over. If he is building on your property, you may agree that it's okay if he's six inches onto your land. But, if you ever sell that home, then the new lender will see that the fence is encroaching on your property and he either won't make a loan on it or he'll require that title insurance leave any claim regarding that fence out of the policy altogether. This could be called a "claim" or "interest" on your property, such that the neighbor might want a piece of it when it comes time to sell. Surveys answer these questions.

Certain parts of the country don't require a survey as drawn by a surveyor and use a different system called "metes and bounds," which is a legal and physical description of the property and all its structures without the use of maps. This description will appear in the title report.

A survey will also show any easements that exist on your property. An easement is a legal right for a third party to access your land whenever he or she feels like it. Common easements are granted for utility companies such as telephone, cable, and electric. If something happened to their power lines and they need to fix them, they can simply go fix them without getting a court order to access your property. It's already been granted by right of an easement.

The Underwriter

Although every one of the players on your team is important, the underwriter is the one who literally says "yes" or "no" to your VA loan request.

Your loan processor gathers up all the documentation required to close your loan, then sends it to this person. Most likely, your loan has already been approved via an AUS. At this stage your loan is delivered to the underwriter, who makes sure that what was asked for by the AUS is not only in the file, but that it meets the AUS requirements.

Most loans are delivered electronically. For instance, when I get ready to turn a loan over to my underwriter, I no longer have to print documents and deliver them to her, but I send the entire file from my computer's loan processing software as a secure attachment. I don't print paper any longer. Most lenders don't, or at least not very much.

If the AUS asks for two pay stubs covering the most recent thirty days, the underwriter will look at your pay stubs to verify that they're from the past thirty days and that they accurately reflect what you say you make. If the loan processor has done her job properly, both of these requirements will be signed off by the underwriter. Sometimes, though, they're not.

Let's say that very early on in your home search you provided two pay stubs covering thirty days, but it took a couple of months to find your dream home. Guess what? Your pay stubs are old. You need to provide new ones that (1) cover the most recent thirty days and (2) match up with what you say you make. It may sound a little dumb to do that, but it's really rather important.

A lot can happen in a couple of months. You can get fired or have your pay cut back or hours reduced. In fact, even when you have your most recent pay stubs in the file, the lender just might make a phone call to your employer and ask for you, or ask to see if you work there. This is known as cross-checking information. Having recent stubs on hand is a normal lending requirement.

If the pay stubs are indeed old, the underwriter won't decline the loan but may instead approve the loan "conditionally." This means the underwriter assumes you're still at the same job making the same amount of money, but before final closing papers are drawn the underwriter will want to see those new stubs.

As well, certain items in your file, called "credit documents," might be old by the time your loan goes to closing. So, again, if your lender asks for thirty days' most recent pay stubs and you're into month two, be prepared to provide a fresh set of stubs that meet the thirty-day requirement.

Whatever is in the file, the underwriter must verify, even if you don't need that item to close your loan.

Escrow Agent or Closing Agent

This is the person who makes sure that all loan papers are signed properly and that the sale took place under the required state laws. This person is the one who authorizes the transfer of money from the buyer to the seller.

In certain parts of the country, this person is called an escrow agent. Elsewhere, he can simply be called the closing agent, or closer.

When lenders deliver closing papers to a closer (again, electronically), there is a piece of paper referencing the "lending instructions" that the closer must follow to the tee. If the lender asks that the buyers sign a copy of their tax returns at closing, the closer makes certain that's done. If the lender asks for copies of a driver's license or passport at closing, the closer makes sure that's done. And so on.

A closing agent can be an attorney in some areas of the country, or from an escrow company in other areas, or from a title company in others. It depends. But however it's done in your state, it's done the same way throughout your state.

Once everything has been done according to law, custom, and the lender's instructions, a sale is consummated. Usually. The loan then goes back to the loan closer or funder.

Funder

Ever heard the expression, "It ain't over till it's over"? Sure you have. Sometimes a lender isn't quite finished with your file. Lenders want to see that their instructions were completed correctly.

Typically a closer will fax or scan/attach signed closing papers back to the funder. The funder reviews those items then provides the closer with a magic number, usually called a "funding number," that is essentially a combination to the safe where the lender has sent the seller's funds.

Sometimes there are Prior to Funding Conditions, called PTFCs. Although these types of conditions are minor and won't hold up closing papers, they are necessary nonetheless. A common PTFC would be an "AKA" statement signed by the buyers. An AKA means "also known as," and it is asked for when somebody signs his or her name differently on different documents.

If William Smith signs his original loan application as Billy Smith but in other places (maybe on his credit report) his name appears as "William R. Smith," then the lender asks for an AKA statement. This is nothing major but will be required to close completely.

Once everything is signed off and approved by the funder, that's when money officially changes hands.

That's your team.

CHAPTER 5

Getting the Best VA Rate

Some of the biggest myths and mysteries involve mortgage interest rates: how they're set, who sets them, where in the heck they come from in the first place. If the VA doesn't issue rates, who does? VA lenders, that's who. And knowing how your VA rate is set will give you the inside track on getting the best deal.

How Interest Rates Are Set

Mortgage rates are not set by the Federal Reserve Board or any other government body. The Fed, among other things, controls the cost of money that banks borrow. Banks borrow money from various sources at one interest rate and then mark that interest rate up a notch or two to the rate at which they lend to their consumer and business customers.

One of the main challenges the Fed undertakes is controlling inflation. It does so by making money more or less expensive to borrow. The more expensive money is—meaning the higher the interest rate— the more the Fed is trying to control inflation.

Inflation is a silent killer of an economy. If a farmer agrees to sell 100 bushels of wheat for $1,000 but after six months that $1,000 is now worth only $900 due to inflation, the farmer loses money. Businesses lose money. The government loses money. And when someone loses money, the natural thing to do to make up for it is . . . to raise prices. But raising prices stokes the flames of inflation. Inflation is such a difficult phenomenon to stop once it gets started. So the Fed tries to make sure it never gets started in the first place.

The Fed meets about once every six weeks to examine lots of things, but primarily to control the cost of money. The Fed attempts to control inflation by controlling the cost of funds—namely, the federal funds rate and the federal discount rate.

The fed funds rate is the rate banks charge one another for short-term lending, usually lending overnight. For anyone who doesn't understand why banks would do that, it's simple if you recall that banks have certain asset-reserve requirements. For every loan issued, a bank must have a predetermined amount of cash sitting in its vaults. This reserve requirement is a direct result of the infamous "bank runs" that helped kick-start the Great Depression.

The Fed also regulates the discount rate, which is the amount set aside for short-term lending that is issued by the federal government directly. Banks can also borrow from the Federal Reserve at discounted rates.

A strong economy is one that is growing at an accelerated rate. A strong economy increases the demand for money because more businesses are willing to borrow more to expand. When the demand for capital increases, lenders can charge more—and they often do. If the economy is not careful, inflation can kick in.

The Fed looks for signs of an improving economy. Lots of new jobs created, lots of new cars being sold, lots of, well, lots of everything good for the economy. If there are too many consecutive signs of a booming economy, the Federal Reserve Board will decide whether to raise fed funds and fed discount rates at its next meeting.

On the other hand, if the economy seems to be going into a slump, or is currently in one, the Fed will do just the opposite . . . lower rates. Lower rates make the cost of money cheaper. If businesses can borrow more money with less cost they'll be encouraged to expand, hire more people, and sell more goods.

You might think, "Hey, I saw the Fed lowered rates yesterday. What kind of rate can I get today?" That's not really how it works. Fixed mortgage rates are set by the open markets, specifically mortgage bonds that are bought and sold throughout every trading day.

Lenders set their mortgage rates based on these mortgage bonds, specifically a Fannie Mae or Ginnie Mae bond.

As the price of these bonds goes up or down, lenders price their mortgage rates accordingly. Mortgage rates are tied to specific bond indexes. Thirty-year rates are tied to a thirty-year mortgage bond index. Fifteen-year rates are tied to a fifteen-year mortgage bond index. Conventional loans and government loans both have their indexes. And it's these bonds being bought and sold by traders—public and private investors—that set market rates.

Since bonds are predictable, the return isn't as sexy as stocks. Instead, bond owners invest because of that guarantee; they don't want any surprises. But who would invest in a mortgage bond when there are other investment opportunities that could pay much more? When the stock market is going crazy and it seems that everyone is investing some amount in stocks to get a great return, then investors typically pull their money out of those staid bonds and use that cash to buy high-flying stocks. Remember the dot-com boom? Real estate? Pet rocks? Betamax?

Bonds must compete for those same investment dollars, and when money pulls out of a mortgage bond to chase higher earnings elsewhere, the seller of those bonds must make adjustments to the price of the bond. When there's less demand, a lower price will be issued. And a lower price means a higher return, or yield, on that bond.

What causes a price to go up or down? The demand. If the stock market is tanking, then investors might want to sell stocks and put more money in the safe return guaranteed by bonds. But if more people want the same thing, then guess what happens? That's right, the price goes up due to increased demand. A bondholder can get more money for the same bond. When the price goes up, the yield, or return, goes down.

Every single day, all day long, there are departments at mortgage companies that do nothing except watch the prices of various mortgage bonds to determine how the companies will set their mortgage rates for the day. These departments are called the "secondary" division of the lender, and every mortgage banking operation has one. It's here that rates are set and distributed to loan officers and, eventually, to you, the borrower.

As each business day opens, all of these secondary departments watch the opening trading of the various mortgage bonds. If the price of the thirty-year Fannie Mae bond is selling on the open market at the same price from yesterday, then rates for that day will be the same.

If the price of the bond goes up, the yield then goes down, meaning rates get lower. If there is less demand for a particular type of mortgage bond, the yield goes up, raising mortgage rates. This goes on all day long. And mortgage prices change constantly.

Mortgage bonds are priced in basis points. One basis point equals one one-hundredth (1/100th) of a percent. As the price of a bond changes throughout the day, the secondary department must be wary of any price swings throughout the day. If the price of a particular mortgage bond moves by just a few basis points, say, three or four, there will be no change.

If, however, there is a move in price of, say, 15 or more basis points, you can expect the lender to make a price adjustment. Different lenders may have different thresholds for price changes, but most will start to get nervous if bond prices have moved one way or another. You can bet if the bond price has changed by 20 or more basis points there will be a midday rate change.

Mostly the rates themselves won't change as much as the cost to the consumer will change. If 6.00 percent can be found at one basis point and mortgage bonds lose 50 basis points, it will typically mean an adjustment in interest rate to 6.125 percent, or one-half discount point more in price. Don't confuse basis points with discount points. They're different. (See the glossary.)

Secondary departments watch mortgage bond pricing and the effect of various economic and political events that might trigger a bond sell-off or a bond rally. Did the Bureau of Labor Statistics unemployment number show strong job gains? Then you can expect money to move from bonds and into stocks. That means higher rates.

Economic events that point to a stronger or weaker economy will affect interest rates throughout the day. So can political events.

Lenders have people to whom they pay a lot of money to set their mortgage rates each day. But because they price their rates from the very same index, there's not a whole lot of difference in rates between one VA lender and another.

VA rates are based on the coupon rate of a mortgage bond called a GNMA. That's the Government National Mortgage Association, and it issues mortgage bonds that trade every business day, all day long, just like any other bond. Lenders peg their VA rates using this type of bond.

That's why it's impossible to find one VA rate at 6.50 percent and another at 6.00 percent on the very same day. This can't happen, so if you see rates advertised and there's a wide gap between them, somebody's lying, and it's probably the one at 6.00 percent.

There's also another way you can tell if the loan officers you're talking to know how and why rates move. If they tell you that rates move with the thirty-year Treasury bond, ten-year Treasury note, or any other kind of instrument, then you might want to question the loan officer's knowledge of the business.

It's like this: You have one shot at this mortgage and you need every advantage you can possibly attain to get the best deal. You'll apply for a mortgage maybe a couple of times in your life, but lenders handle mortgages all the time, every day. If you close on your loan and made a mistake, there's no recourse.

Lenders do, however, know that it's a competitive market, and they must price their loans as such or their loan officers will never get any deals because their company's rates are so darned high.

Understand that "high rates" are a relative term. Higher rates don't mean a 0.5 percent variance, but instead something a tad more minuscule—typically no more than one-eighth of a percent between VA lender A and VA lender B. Usually it's less than that.

Often a lender variance might be something as small as one-quarter of a discount point. We'll discuss closing costs in more detail in Chapter 6, but a discount point is one percent of the loan amount. For a $300,000 loan, one point equals $3,000. One-quarter point on a $300,000 loan is $750. That's how close lenders can be when pricing their VA loans.

With all this volatility in mortgage rates, you can easily understand this next principle: Interest rates you see in the newspaper are rarely reliable and, in fact, are typically nothing more than an advertisement with a phone number.

I know that sounds a little goofy, but you can't reserve that interest rate, and no lender is going to give it to you simply because it's printed in the paper or on some website somewhere. There will most usually be some disclaimer such as, "Rates and terms subject to change without notice, blah, blah, blah."

Ads are designed to do nothing more than get the phone to ring. Because rates can change from day to day—and indeed throughout the day—then rates found in the paper are already old, even if they were reliable in all cases. Newspapers usually require that interest rate advertisements be sent into their ad department no later than Thursday for entry in Sunday's newspapers. Yes, you can "compare" different rates from one lender to the next, but you can't count on them.

What you can count on is that they are trying to get you to call them to get their rates.

Rate Negotiation with Your Loan Officer

Now that you know how rates are set by lenders, how do you get the best rate? Let me throw in a real big loop at this point: Even though lenders set their own interest rates, the individual loan officer you're working with will set your ultimate rate.

Confusing? Not really. If you understand how mortgage loan officers are paid, then you'll understand completely.

Mortgage loan officers get paid on commission. No loan, no paycheck. Chicken one day, feathers the next.

When you work with a mortgage broker, each and every day that mortgage broker pores over those wholesale rate sheets looking for the lowest rate possible. Because rates are so close together from one lender to the next, a loan officer will rarely find one lender offering 6.25 percent and another 6.00 percent. Instead, the loan officer will find a lender who charges less for each particular rate.

For instance, Lender A offers 6 percent at one discount point while Lender B offers the very same loan at 0.875 percent discount point, or one-eighth of a percent less than one full discount point. On a $300,000 loan, that one-eighth of a percent is $375 in difference between the two wholesale lenders.

If the mortgage broker quotes you one point and a $3,000 origination charge for a 6 percent loan, the broker will most likely choose the wholesale lender offering 6 percent at 0.875 discount point. Now, on that same $300,000 loan, the broker makes not just the $3,000 origination charge, but also the extra $375 in one-eighth point difference.

Or more dramatically, the mortgage loan officer will take that 6.00 percent rate and bump it up by one-eighth of a percent to 6.125 percent. Typically, a one-eighth of a percent jump in rate yields about as much as one-half discount point does. On a $300,000 loan, that one-half point results in another $1,500. Instead of quoting you 6.00 percent, the loan officer might quote you 6.125 percent instead, hoping other factors in his offerings lure you to his mortgage company. Instead of $375, the loan officer attempts to make $1,500.

Rates set by wholesale lenders are just that . . . wholesale, and it's the mortgage broker who ultimately sets your rate, not the lender. The loan officer is simply determining how much money he'll make on your VA loan.

How do mortgage bankers, then, set their rates? Under the very same format, lenders publish their rates for distribution to their legion of loan officers, who take those rates, then mark them up to meet retail, or street-level, mortgage rates.

The only difference at this stage is that the mortgage banking loan officer can only rely on her own mortgage company to issue a base rate. This base rate is what the mortgage bank requires. If a mortgage bank offers 6 percent at no points and the loan officer gives that rate to his borrower, then the loan officer makes no money. He didn't mark it up to make any income. He essentially worked for free.

Don't expect this to happen. At least not on purpose. Mortgage banks will issue a daily rate sheet to their loan officers, and the loan officers have some latitude as what to quote their customers and still make a living. There are typically three basic mortgage banking retail pricing structures:

1. Mortgage Bank Minimum
2. Retail Minimum
3. Retail Required

Under a Mortgage Bank Minimum, the lender issues its VA rate and says to the loan officer, "Hey, here's what we've got, go out and make some loans. Just make sure we get what we ask for."

In this scenario, lenders could issue a VA rate of 6.50 percent at zero points to their loan officers. Loan officers could then quote that rate to the VA customer at 6.50 percent at one point and keep the point or split it with their employer at their agreed-upon rate, or even offer 6.50 percent at one-half point.

Whatever the loan officer quotes and gets, that's what gets sent to the mortgage banker. The mortgage company's secondary department gets its required 6.50 percent at no points; the loan officer gets whatever she got on top of that. I've seen loan officers make absolutely nothing on a loan. Usually by mistake, but it happens. As long as the mortgage bank made its minimum, the loan will go through.

Under a Retail Minimum structure, the mortgage bank says, "Here's my 6.50 percent at zero points, but you must charge a minimum of one discount point or origination charge for us to split."

This pricing method is the result of a loan officer commission-split agreement. A lender will hire loan officers and agree to split the proceeds from the discount point, origination charges, or other lender fees, but the loan officer must also agree to charge a minimum to the borrower, most often one percent of the loan amount.

If the loan officer doesn't charge the consumer a one percent origination or discount point, the loan officer will give up all proceeds to her employer. That's the incentive to charge the minimum. No minimum, no paycheck.

On the other hand, if a loan officer charges two points on a loan, the lender and the loan officer split the total amount charged. On a $300,000 loan with two points, the lender makes 2 percent of $300,000, or $6,000.

With a Retail Required pricing structure, the loan officer has no choice as to what to quote the borrower; it's dictated by the mortgage company. Most usually this is the case with retail banking institutions.

When you walk into your bank to cash a check or make a deposit or whatever, you'll see signs on the wall or a marquee set up somewhere that says, "Thirty-year fixed-rate mortgage 6 percent and one point," or something similar. You walk in, apply for a loan, and get what the bank says you'll get. The loan officer is simply there to take your loan application, not negotiate your rate.

These three pricing scenarios can come in a variety of formats.

Your credit union could set mortgage pricing in one format or another. It depends. In fact, depending on how the pricing structure is established, you could get different rate quotes from different branches of the same bank.

For lenders who use Retail or Mortgage Bank Minimum, it's the loan officer who sets the final price to the consumer, not the bank. That means you could call a loan officer at one branch for a rate quote and call still another and get a different rate quote because the loan officers have pricing latitude . . . they're given a wholesale price and then they're marking it up so that they can make as much money as possible while still getting the loan.

After all, if a loan officer marks the loan up too much, she won't get the deal; the veteran will find a better deal somewhere else. The loan officer must act like any other business and walk the fine line of quoting a competitive rate while at the same time making money. No one works for free. At least not for very long.

This is probably the most misunderstood aspect of mortgage rates: Mortgage lenders don't set the rates—ultimately, the loan officer does.

One note here about direct lenders and mortgage bankers: There is an inherent advantage a banker has that a broker does not, and that's the time advantage.

Bankers can work more quickly at putting your loan through the different stages than a broker can. I recall how I learned this several years ago, when I changed from being a mortgage broker to a mortgage banker.

There are tons of paperwork involved in a VA loan, all with various terms and words you're not familiar with. And you're trying to close within a set period of time, which makes rushing through documents all the more likely to produce mistakes. Mistakes happen. The important thing is to understand how mistakes are fixed.

When I lived in San Diego and worked as a mortgage broker, once in a while there would be an error on the closing papers. Someone's name would be misspelled, for example. Loan documents can't close with names that are wrong. Your attorney or closing agent can't simply line through the incorrect spelling and replace it with the new one. No, new papers have to be drawn up. When a mistake was found, I contacted the wholesale lender and tracked down my customer service

representative or called my loan processor, telling her that we needed
to redraw closing papers.

Unfortunately, a wholesale lender can rarely simply redraw "your"
closing papers at the drop of a hat. That lender has perhaps hundreds,
or maybe even thousands, of closing papers to be drawn. That redraw
request would take one to two days . . . even if it was the mistake of
the wholesale lender and not mine. I would have to call my processor,
then my processor has to call our customer service representative, who
calls the lender, who contacts the closing department, who puts the
loan in line for new papers to redraw then send to the closing agent.

That takes time and it's not fun.

When I moved to Austin, Texas, and became a mortgage banker,
I saw one of my first loans that had a mistake on it. The loan amount
was incorrect. This was one of my first deals in Texas and I was freak-
ing out. So I called my processor and told her what was going on. She
told me to call the document department. I did, and told the document
department that the loan amount was wrong. They said, "Okay, we'll
fix it." And they redrew the closing papers right then and sent them to
the title company for closing. Within an hour.

Bankers have an inherent edge in control of the lending process.
Brokers might be able to squeeze out another one-eighth of a percent
in rate—which is no small feat—but they lose some of the control that
bankers have.

Finding the Best Rate

Mortgage rate quotes can be very confusing, and I'll bet the bevy of
loan officers do that on purpose to confuse you.

Fortunately for VA loans, there is usually only one mortgage loan
product . . . fixed. And that's a huge benefit for you. Every now and
then, when Congress appropriates funds for various government
agencies, they can also put in some allowances for adjustable-rate
mortgages. They don't do it every year, but sometimes they do.

What's the difference between fixed and adjustable mortgages?

Fixed-Rate Loans

The fixed mortgage doesn't change. Loan terms for VA fixed-rate mortgages are typically fifteen and thirty years. The longer the term, the

lower the payment but the higher the interest rate. If you borrow $100,000 over thirty years, you might get a rate at 6.50 percent, for example. The difference in rate for fifteen and thirty years is, on average, about one-quarter of a percent. If you can get a 6.50 percent thirty-year VA note, then you could also get a fifteen-year fixed VA note at 6.25 percent at about the same cost.

Because the payoff period for fifteen-year loans is squished in half, there's a lower interest rate. You are paying less interest, but you're paying off $100,000 twice as fast as a thirty-year loan. That means you'll have to pay a little more each month.

On a thirty-year note at 6.50 percent and $100,000, the monthly payment works out to $629 per month. For a similar fifteen-year mortgage at 6.25 percent and $100,000, the monthly payment blossoms to $853. That's a lot. But that's the difference between fifteen and thirty years.

There's one neat thing worth noting, though: You can pay extra on your mortgage at any time with a VA loan. That means that even though your thirty-year mortgage payment might be $629, you can always pay ahead on the principal and pay off your mortgage sooner. Just because you have a thirty-year VA loan doesn't mean you're forced to pay it off over thirty years. You can pay if off as soon as you want and can afford to.

ARMs

Adjustable-rate mortgages, or ARMs, can inherently adjust. There are three key figures in ARMs: the index, the margin, and the caps.

The interest rates on most ARMs you'll see can adjust once per year and are based on the one-year Treasury note. This note is your index. The other significant piece of an ARM is the margin, which is the number added to your index to give you your "fully indexed rate" or the new rate your payment will be based upon for the coming year.

Each year, on your anniversary date, you'll notice the interest rate can adjust once again. Forever. Or at least until you pay off your loan.

For instance, let's say the one-year Treasury note is at 5.00 percent. A standard margin is 2.75 percent. When you add those two numbers together you get $5.00 + 2.75 = 7.75$ percent. Your interest rate is 7.75 percent for the coming year.

VA ARMs—when they're available, anyway—have a neat consumer feature called "caps." A cap is a limit that your rate may not exceed, regardless of the index. This cap is usually one percent above your previous mortgage rate.

Let's now say one year has passed and the one-year Treasury is at 8.00 percent instead of 5.00 percent. Now, by adding the 2.75 margin, your fully indexed rate is 10.75 percent. That's a full 3.00 percent above your previous year's rate.

On a $100,000 note, 7.75 percent gives you a $712 monthly payment, whereas 10.75 percent is $933 per month! However, because you have a one percent cap, although the rate wants to go to 10.75 percent, it will only go up one percent over the previous year's rate. If you started at 5.00 percent and your fully indexed rate was at 7.75 percent, because of the cap, it would only go to 7.00 percent, or a payment of $665.

VA ARMs aren't issued very often; in fact, they were really only an experiment for a few years. Because they may come back at any time, I want to review them to explain how they work.

When they're available, should you take an ARM over a fixed rate?

ARMs typically have a unique feature called a "teaser" rate, which is artificially low at the start. For example, an ARM might start out at 5.50 percent, yet its fully indexed rate might be closer to 6.50 percent or 7.00 percent, which is tempting to take.

Compare what current fixed-rate loans are offering. If a fixed rate is one or two percent above your teaser rate, I would suggest the fixed rate. Teasers are artificially low and will go to the fully indexed rate typically at year one or year two, where a fixed rate was all along.

Historically, it's good to consider an ARM when rates are at relative highs and a fixed rate when rates are at relative lows. Over the past few years, interest rates have stabilized and haven't been as wild as they were over the past couple of decades. Probably the best resource to check historical interest rates is at a website called HSH Associates, or www.hsh.com.

Another reason to consider an ARM is that you might only be owning the property for a very short period of time, say, two to three years. In that case, take the ARM. You'll get the teaser rate for the first year and then be cap-protected for the next couple of years.

One word of caution: As anyone knows, plans can change. Sometimes when you thought you would be moving soon, you find out you won't be. Perhaps your job plans change, or you decide to retire. If your plans change, can you handle the higher rate?

I've never been a fan of ARMs in any environment. That's probably nothing more than a personality trait of mine. I'm just not a gambler by nature, and an ARM is in effect some sort of a gamble. But with a fixed rate, there is no gamble. You always know what your rate will be and you can plan on it.

Start your rate search with an institution you know or have a current relationship with. Most likely that will be your bank or credit union. Although you may not end up there, you can use it as a benchmark. Then contact two or more mortgage brokers or mortgage bankers.

It's important to first decide on your mortgage type and stick with it. If you want a thirty-year fixed, stick with it. Don't let a loan officer talk you into a fifteen-year mortgage. It's important to go into the rate-shopping game with one goal: to get the best rate on the loan you want. Don't be led astray.

Now, get your phone numbers and a piece of paper, pour yourself a cup of coffee, and start calling. Do not rely on websites to give you rate quotes. You want a live quote from a real person, not a bait-and-switch tactic.

Don't bother calling until about noon Eastern Time. That's because lenders wait to watch the credit markets open and see how the GNMA bond is doing that morning. Once the bond is pegged, pricing will begin to roll out to the various VA lenders and their loan officers.

You also need to determine the length of time you're going to need to get your rate quote for. Most often, it will be for a thirty-day period, a typical closing cycle for a home purchase.

If you're buying a home that's not finished yet and the home's not going to be ready for another three months or so, a thirty-day rate quote won't do you any good. The longer the guarantee, or "lock" period, the more it's going to cost you.

A loan officer can quote you 6.00 percent for thirty days, but if you needed to lock that in for sixty days, the loan officer will either increase your rate by one-eighth of a percent to 6.125 percent or charge you another one-quarter discount point to extend that rate. Longer locks cost more.

As do shorter locks. Lenders also offer ten-day or fifteen-day lock periods. But unless your loan is already approved with that lender and all your paperwork is completed, then a ten- or fifteen-day lock is useless.

That's a common trick among loan officers who quote rates. You call up and ask for their VA rate and they'll tell you something like 5.75 percent while everyone else is at 6.00 percent. (Suspicious already, right?) But he can't close you because he doesn't have your loan application, and that rate is only good for people already in his pipeline.

So you think you've found the lowest lender on the planet only to discover that mysteriously his VA rate is the same as everyone else's—in fact, it just might be higher. Don't fall for this tactic. It's too common.

Call your selected loan officer and say: "Please give me your thirty-year VA rate with no points and no origination charges, and I need a thirty-day lock quote, please. My loan amount is $250,000."

Lenders can adjust their rates slightly given higher or lower loan amounts. If loans are less than $50,000, for instance, a lender might charge an additional one-eighth discount point. If it's higher than $200,000, then you might get a little discount. But whichever it is, make the exact same request to each lender.

It's also critical that you make your rate-quote telephone calls at the same time of day, because rates can move about during the course of a business day. In the morning rates might be one-quarter of a point lower than they were in the afternoon. If you made calls to two lenders in the morning and two late in the afternoon, you might find that the afternoon lenders were much lower than the morning ones. You didn't just hit the jackpot. The markets likely moved during the course of the day and everyone lowered their rates. You can't assume the morning lenders were simply higher; they just quoted you current rates. If you discover a discrepancy, you need to contact those other lenders again to get a current quote. If you don't, it won't be fair to you or the loan officers you're talking to.

Let's say that after a couple of days of checking VA rates, you've nailed down two people you like. Their rates are the same and their fees are the same. You like both loan officers, and both of them have returned all your e-mails and phone calls promptly.

If you're that close to finding the best rate and best lender, then either one will work for you. At this point, you might even decide to go to the person you like more. It might be a personality issue. If both loan officers are quoting the exact same thing, then you want to choose someone you'll enjoy working with over the next thirty days. If your personalities fit, why not choose the person you like more?

Sounds odd to base a lender choice on whom you like most, but if all things are equal and you've nailed the two best rates in town, then work with someone who'll put a smile on your face or say "Yes, sir" or "No, ma'am" when you ask him a question.

Rate Locks

Some lenders may quote you a great rate, but they won't allow you to lock that rate in unless you have a loan application with them. In fact, I don't know of any lender that will allow you that luxury.

If you're going to lock in your VA rate with a lender, a lender also wants to see if you're serious as well, or if you are just shopping around.

When you lock in a rate, that lender also locks in that rate for you with its wholesale lender, in the case of a mortgage broker, or reserves your loan in its credit line so that no one else can get to it. If a lender has a $100 million credit line and you want to lock in your VA rate at 5 percent for a $400,000 loan, then that lender will literally put your name on $400,000 of that credit line. It's reserved especially for you at the rate you locked in.

If you change your mind or otherwise don't close your loan with that lender, then the lender has to put that money back in the till. It's made a commitment based upon your request and perhaps lost money on that commitment if someone else wanted to lock in at those rates but couldn't because that rate was no longer available in that $100 million pool of funds.

Locks are serious business. It costs lenders money when buyers break locks or don't close with them when they thought they would.

Paying Points

Points, or discount points, are a form of prepaid mortgage interest. Mortgage interest can be tax-deductible, and if points are mortgage interest, they're tax-deductible also. Paying points to get a lower rate is called a permanent buydown.

Paying a point, or one percent of your loan amount, should result in decreasing your mortgage rate by one-quarter of a percent. If you can get 7.25 percent at zero points, then you should also be able to find 7.00 percent with one point. Or 6.75 percent at two points. Here's how you decide whether to pay points.

First, take the no-point option and calculate the monthly payment. On a $250,000 loan at 7.25 percent over thirty years, the monthly payment is $1,695. No points.

A loan at 7.00 percent at one point costs $2,500 and also drops your monthly payment to $1,653. A loan at 6.75 percent at two points or $5,000 reduces your payment still more to the tune of $1,612.

Subtract the difference in monthly payments, then divide that amount into the point dollar amount. This figure will give you the number of months it would take to "recover" your investment in paying points.

For instance, 7.25 percent and 7.00 percent have payments of $1,695 and $1,653, respectively, or a difference of $42 per month, yet you paid $2,500 in points. That $2,500 divided by $42 equals 59.5 months. After the fifty-ninth month, you will see a reward in paying that point from that "point" forward.

Further still, the difference between 7.25 percent and 6.75 percent or $1,695 and $1,612, is $83 per month. Divide the $5,000 in points by $83 and you get a return in month 60.

Am I a fan of points? No. The resulting lower payment is usually not low enough to offset the additional charge. If you can live with getting your point "back" in five years, then go right ahead.

Remember that a point is a potential tax deduction for those who itemize, but it can also be said that the very same point could be put to better use by investing in the stock market or a mutual fund or something else. Or maybe that $5,000 could have gone toward a nice new range for the home and maybe a matching fridge and dishwasher.

Personally, knowing me, I wouldn't put $5,000 into a money market fund anyway, but I would buy new stuff for the house if it needed it instead. But on the other side of the coin, there are people who would say that the $5,000 put into a retirement account or some other savings vehicle is the better choice. They're probably right, but I don't think it's a clear-cut choice.

This point trade-off exercise is better viewed this way: If you don't get your interest rate reduced by one-quarter of a percent when you pay a point, you might be getting a raw deal. If you get a no-point rate at 7.25 percent but one point gets you only 7.125 percent and not 7.00 percent, then don't do it.

Or if you get a 7.00 percent rate at one point but 6.875 percent at two points, then don't do that, either. If you're getting quoted three points on anything, run away.

If you decide to lock in that day and get 7.25 percent at zero points but change your mind later, deciding that you want to pay a point to get 7.00 percent, then you'll have to settle for the pricing for the day you locked in at, not the pricing for the day you changed your mind.

If your thirty-day rate at 7.25 percent expires, then you'll typically be subject to worse-case pricing . . . you'll get the higher of whatever you locked in at or current market rates.

Lenders can also offer rate lock extensions if you or your loan officer observe that your rate might expire before your loan can close. Extensions are typically only issued before a rate expires and not afterward. This ensures that you get the better rates if rates have moved up since you locked in.

For instance, you lock in at 7.25 percent for thirty days and your builder tells you that it's going to be another ten days before the house is completed. In the meantime, mortgage rates have moved up to 7.75 percent, a full one-half of a percent above what you locked in. On day 31, if you don't get an extension, it's possible your new rate will be much higher, at 7.75 percent. However, if you get a rate lock extension on or before day 30, you might still keep your 7.25 percent rate, if only for a few days.

Rate lock extensions will cost you a little money, usually about one-quarter of a point for another fifteen days, sometimes one-eighth of a point for five days. But in this example, if your rate could go to 7.75

percent, then it makes sense to pay the extra one-quarter point to keep your lower, locked-in rate.

For instance, on a $250,000 loan at 7.25 percent, the payment is $1,705 compared to the $1,791 payment at 7.75 percent. If you needed ten more days and extended it a safe fifteen days at one-quarter point, or $625, you've won. That $86 difference in monthly payment will be recovered in seven months.

You can tell lenders get serious about rate locks, maybe even more serious than you realize. Blown locks and rate miscalculations can cost them millions of dollars.

What if you locked in and rates move down after you've locked in? Well, you're stuck. If you have a purchase contract and you're supposed to close within thirty days and you've got twenty-five days left, you might find out that rates have gone down after you got your thirty-day lock.

If that happens, call your loan officer and ask for the new, lower rate. You'll meet some resistance, especially if your rate has only gone down one-eighth of a percent or so. Still, the difference between 7.00 percent and 7.125 percent equals $7,059 over 30 years on a $200,000 loan. Don't count on getting the new rate, but at least you have to ask.

With one-eighth of a percent drop in rate, your loan officer most likely will do nothing. He is not responsible for setting lock-in policy for the lender. Your lender has already reserved your interest rate for you and moved on. However, if rates have moved one-quarter of a percent or more since you locked in yours, you may have the upper hand. Lenders know that you probably won't change lenders just for one-eighth of a percent, but you very well might for one-quarter or especially one-half of a percent. You can threaten to pull the loan if you don't get the answer you want, and lenders might be willing to change the rate to keep the loan.

It's a gamble on both ends. If you threaten to move your loan to another lender, you run the risk of not closing on time with the new lender because you essentially have to start all over again. The lender will need to order another appraisal, loan applications must be completed (another reason to apply at more than one VA lender), and a new set of VA disclosures must be signed and returned.

In fact, if rates do go down, you can expect a phone call from the loan officer who wasn't so lucky to get your loan in the first place, saying, "Hey, David, just wanted to let you know that rates have dropped by another one-half of a percent. Call me. I still think we have time to close your loan!"

If you're a couple of weeks away, it's probably too late to change lenders. If you're two weeks away from closing, the lender you originally locked in with won't change your rate . . . the lender knows you run the risk of not making your closing date and losing the house altogether. If you're three weeks or more out, it's probable that you'll meet your closing date and still get the new rate, so the lender might think twice and renegotiate a rate with you. Maybe.

If your current lender flinches, he'll likely make a counteroffer that may not give you the entire one-half of a percent but part of it, because he wants to keep the loan in-house. Otherwise, losing a loan before it funds will cost the lender money, especially after all the work that has already been done on your loan.

Buydowns

Another form of a buydown that is available on your VA loan is the temporary buydown, so called because your start rate is temporarily lower than what the current market is offering yet will eventually creep up to market rates.

It works like this: During year one of your mortgage, your rate could be 4 percent, then the next year it will automatically increase one percentage point to 5 percent, then the next year it will up one more percent to 6 percent, then stay there for the remaining term of your loan.

This buydown is called a 2–1 buydown. Your market rate is 6 percent, yet you go down 2 percent the first year, then one percent the second. If you're at 7 percent, the 2–1 buydown would mean you start at 5 percent, then go to 6 percent, then finally to 7 percent and remain there.

There are other buydowns called 3–2–1 buydowns that act the very same way, except they start 3 percent below the note rate, and so on.

Why bother? For one thing, you get qualified at the start rate instead of the final note rate. If you're pushing debt ratios or you're seeing a house you want that is ever so slightly out of your reach, then consider a buydown.

For instance, on a $250,000 thirty-year loan, 7 percent gives you a $1,653 per month payment, yet the start rate on a 2–1 buydown at 5 percent is just $1,336. That's a lot. And it can help qualify you for more home because your qualifying rate is a full two percentage points below your original note rate.

Or, even if you are already qualified at the 7 percent rate, it simply gives you a lower monthly payment for a couple of years, letting you take the money you would have otherwise spent on your house payment and use it for other things.

One note of caution here: Don't get a buydown just to get qualified at the start rate without having made adjustments for the higher payments later on down the road. Nothing is fun about foreclosure. If payments get too high, that's what can happen if you no longer can afford your home.

Use a buydown if you anticipate increased earnings over the next few years, such as a raise or pension, or if you're getting married to someone who also works or will have other forms of income to offset the higher payments.

But if you can swing it and would like the lower start rates, then ask your VA loan officer to calculate a buydown for you. Yes, I said calculate.

There's a trade-off between getting a regular thirty-year fixed rate at 6 percent and considering a 2–1 buydown where the loan actually starts 2 percent lower the first year. The lender is losing some interest there, no? Guess who pays for it . . . you do. And here's how to calculate it.

Take the difference in interest from the 6 percent rate and the 4 percent and 5 percent rate, and then divide that by your loan amount. That number will be in decimal form and is the number of points it will take to subsidize the buydown.

Example. On a $250,000 loan, 4 percent is $1,193 and 5 percent is $1,342 but the permanent note rate of 6 percent is $1,471. Your interest payments over twelve months would break down as follows:

Rate	Months	Interest
4.00%	12	$ 9,919
5.00%	12	$12,416
6.00%	12	$14,916

By adding up the interest over the first two years, the amount is $22,335. However, if the note rate had been at 6 percent over those same two years, it would add up to about $29,643.

Now subtract the lower interest paid amount of $22,335 from the $29,643.

$$\$29,643—\$22,335 = \$7,308$$

That's the amount of interest the lender "lost" during that time frame.

To calculate the buydown, divide $7,308 by your loan amount of $250,000 and the answer is .0292, or 2.92 in points. You will pay the lender at closing 2.92 points for your buydown.

There is one more twist to a temporary buydown, and it's called a "lender funded" buydown. It's called lender funded because you don't pay the points; instead, the lender adjusts the rate for you.

But again, it's not free. The lender will adjust your note rate up by about one-half of a percent instead of you paying about two points. In this example, your lender-funded buydown would instead be 6.50 percent, 5.50 percent, and 4.50 percent. You paid for it, not the lender, but you paid for it in the form of a higher rate.

Applying to More Than One Lender

Lenders make money. That's their job. But their job is also to make certain the money they've committed to their borrowers actually comes through. During all the shenanigans of computing buydowns or paying points, lenders lose money if they do all that and don't close your deal.

Lenders make nothing unless your loan closes with them.

That's why lenders aren't all that keen on issuing interest rate guarantees to people who don't even have an application in with them. So what do you do? Why not apply with more than one lender?

It's okay. Really. There is no law that says you can't, and your credit score won't get pounded because you've got a mortgage application in at two or three lenders. This is actually the only way you can make sure you're getting quoted the best interest rate while also being able to guarantee that rate via a rate lock.

When you apply at more than one company, there's no reason to supply them with all your documentation up front. Instead, just fill out your loan application and worry about everything else, especially your Certificate of Eligibility, later. You can begin gathering anticipated documentation, such as your pay stubs or insurance information, but don't submit it to any lender until you've decided who you're going to use as your VA lender.

One additional hurdle you may run into is that the lender may require that you pay your money for the appraisal before locking anything in. Although that's not an uncommon request, it shouldn't be just to lock in a loan.

Lenders can have their own internal policies that vary from one company to the next, and sometimes you'll have to swallow a bad policy you don't like. If you love your chosen VA lender, then go ahead and pay for your appraisal if that's what the lender requires.

But if you have two VA lenders that are quoting similar terms, work with the less stringent lender.

If you're serious about your rate lock and you're determined to work with the lender you locked in at, you should be able to send in your appraisal money without regard to a rate lock. Again, lenders want to make sure you're serious and not still rate shopping.

And this is important . . . once you make a decision to go with a particular lender, stay with that lender. An escrow period or contract period is typically thirty days, and you don't have a lot of time to bounce from lender to lender.

This is especially true with your VA loan. It's your chosen lender or mortgage broker who will order the Certificate of Eligibility. It's your lender who will order the Notice of Value, or NOV. All your loan documents will have the lender's name on them. If you change mortgage companies midstream, you can run out of time, potentially losing the home you really want to buy.

Although VA loans don't necessarily take longer to get approved, it may take longer to switch lenders compared to other loan types available on the market. Do your homework, pick a lender, and stick with it.

Unless the lender completely screws everything up, of course.

What if you get to your closing and you discover that your interest rate of 6.50 percent magically changed to 6.75 percent . . . or worse? When you're at the closing table and you find that out, it might be a little late. You can't close that day. Everything has to be changed and redrawn by your lender. If you used a mortgage broker and the loan papers are wrong, then that adds another couple of days before you can close due to the communication lag between lender and broker.

The first thing you should have done is gotten a copy of your "lock-in agreement" issued by your lender. This agreement spells out exactly what your mortgage rate will be and how long that lock is good for.

Do not accept verbals on lock in agreements. You need a signed form, in your hands. If you lock in with your loan officer, you need to tell her on the phone, "Okay, lock me in for thirty days at 5.50 percent today and send me your lock confirmation." Make sure you get it in writing. When you go to your closing, take your lock agreement with you in case the rate is wrong.

Another way to avoid getting the wrong rate at closing is to demand to review all your closing documents one day before you close. This way you can review them at your home or work and ask questions before your closing, instead of or in addition to while you're at closing. This makes for a more peaceful closing, trust me.

Do lenders really change rates on borrowers without them knowing? Some probably do, and it's usually not the lender but the loan officer trying to pull a fast one on you. It doesn't happen very often but it happens. I've seen it.

Loan officers who pull this bait-and-switch trick won't be in business for very long, or if they have been, they don't get much referral business. That's why getting referrals for your loan officer is crucial. You need someone with a strong reputation who relies on repeat business.

CHAPTER 6

Closing Costs and VA Loans

Closing costs are an inherent piece of the VA loan process, or any mortgage loan, for that matter. But the difference with a VA loan is that there are restrictions as to what you, as the veteran or qualifying VA borrower, can and cannot pay.

Every other loan program, including the VA's sister loan program, the FHA loan, can have closing cost responsibilities negotiated. In some cases, customs are already established as to who pays for what, the buyer or the seller.

But with a VA loan, there are hard rules as to what closing costs you can pay for and what costs cannot be charged to you as a veteran. This is another huge advantage of VA home loans.

First, though, let's break down home loan closing costs into two distinct categories: recurring and nonrecurring closing fees. Recurring means they'll happen again. Nonrecurring means they won't.

A recurring closing cost is something that you'll pay either monthly or annually for the life of the loan. A good example is home-owners insurance. Although you'll pay for a policy for one full year at your closing, you'll have to renew it again in twelve months. It occurs again.

Another recurring closing cost is property taxes. Taxes are due annually in most states, and in some states they are due semiannually. Either way, as long as you own that property, you'll pay them again.

Interest is still another recurring cost. Interest is part of your loan agreement and you'll pay it every time you make a mortgage payment.

If you buy into a condominium project or other managed property that has a homeowner's association, you'll pay those fees over and over. Either every year or every month.

Recurring costs aren't something that will change when you compare one lender to the next. After all, the lender has nothing to do with your property taxes, your insurance, or your homeowner's association dues.

Saving Money on Closing Costs

One way to save on recurring closing costs is by adjusting your closing date. In reality, you're not "saving" anything but instead are affecting your cash flow.

Mortgage interest payments are the direct opposite of rent payments. When you pay rent, you're paying for the month you're about to live in your apartment or unit. When you pay mortgage interest, you're paying it in "arrears," meaning you're paying the lender for the number of days you've already owned the property. That little "quirk" in how mortgage interest is paid actually helps you conserve a little cash when it comes to closing time. How's that?

When you go to sign your closing papers, you'll see an item on your settlement statement that lists all of your and your seller's closing expenses. On line item 901, you'll see a section that lists "Interest for XX days @ $##.## per day." This is the entry for prepaid interest. When you close, your closing agent will include this charge, and it is in effect your first month's housing payment . . . with a twist.

Your prepaid interest charges are added up for each day until the first of the following month. Here's how it works: Your daily, or per diem, interest is calculated from the day you sign your closing papers and take possession of the property until the first of the following month.

If you close on the twentieth of the month, your lender will calculate your per diem interest up to the first of the following month. If you have a $300,000 loan at 7 percent on a thirty-year note, your daily interest charge would be about $58.33 per day.

Now count how many days there are from the twentieth to the first of the following month and you get ten days—or eleven if the month you close has thirty-one days instead of thirty. Ten days times $66.00 equals $660. That's an amount you'll need to come in with as a recurring cost (mortgage interest) and that you'll need to plan for.

But because mortgage interest is paid in arrears and not in advance, you will "skip" your first month's house payment and not have a payment due until the second month after you close.

Let's say you close your loan on January 25 and your per diem interest is $44.00 per day. The closing agent will collect on the lender's behalf seven days' worth of interest, from January 25 through January 31, or $308. Now, because mortgage interest is paid in arrears, your February house payment of $308 (the interest portion) was already made at your closing. You won't write a check for your "first" house payment until March.

Although it "feels" like you skipped a mortgage payment, you didn't . . . you paid it at closing in the form of prepaid interest. This is where saving money comes into play.

Because you prepay interest at your closing, when you close affects how much your interest charges will be. If you close on the second of the month, the lender will want twenty-eight days of interest; if you close on the last day of the month, the lender will want just one day.

With $66 per diem interest, twenty-eight days is $1,848 and one day is, well, $66. That's a big difference and something you have partial control over by selecting your closing date. That's why you'll hear people tell you to close at the end of the month to reduce your closing costs.

In effect, you are reducing your costs, but actually if you take ownership of a property on the second and not on the last day of the month, you're still paying the same thing, if you consider when you actually own the property. If you own for twenty-eight days, you'll pay the respective interest. You own sooner. It doesn't "cost" you more, it just affects your cash flow. You own sooner, you pay more. If you want to save cash by closing on the last day of the month, you'll save a lot.

On a side note, there can be dangers in closing on the very last day of a month. Because everyone else buying real estate wants to close at the end of the month to save interest charges, that means the bulk of closings take place in the course of a very few days. It also means your lender begins to work overtime toward the end of the month to handle the additional workload. Sometimes people who work in the loan closing department of a lender wonder, "Why do people always want to close at the very same time!" when the answer is that people are all trying to do the very same thing—save on interest charges.

When things get so crazy toward the end of the month, the lender can get backlogged. What happens if when you go to the closing you find your name is misspelled on the paperwork? Or the property address is wrong . . . or some other mistake? Unfortunately, the closing agent can't pull out a bottle of Wite-Out® and write the correct name in all the correct places.

No, your loan closing papers have to be redrawn all over again. By your lender. And it would truly be a miracle if you got those same closing papers out for that same day. Why would it be a miracle? Because lenders' closing departments are bogged down. That means if you wanted to save as much money as possible for your closing and waited until the very last day, you could wind up paying much, much more than you would if the closing were held on the second or third day of the following month, when your lender is most likely to get a new set of closing papers out to your closing agent.

If you want to save some pocket change, go ahead and close during the last part of the month, but don't close on the last day of the month. People can make mistakes. You need to anticipate that mistakes might happen and schedule your closing toward the end of the month with a few days to spare.

I always advise my clients to schedule their closings on or around the twenty-fifth of the month. That's far enough out to save significant prepaid interest charges, you're closing before most everyone else is, and if there are errors on any of your closing papers, the lender is staffed up enough to fix the error quickly. Let everybody else try to shove their deals through at the very last minute. Buying a home can be stressful enough as it is without adding to the mix with a last-day closing.

Saving on Nonrecurring Fees

Nonrecurring fees are the ones you should be most concerned about. Those are the costs you'll be paying once—but having to pay, nonetheless—and they are the fees that have the possibility of being negotiated down or eliminated altogether. They're also the fees that can be manipulated by a loan officer when getting quotes from lenders that make them appear to be a better deal than their VA competitors.

Although every state, and even sometimes every county or parish, can have different closing fees, common nonrecurring fees charged by your "team" can add up to a lot. Typical nonrecurring fees work out as follows:

Appraisal/NOV	$350
Attorney	$200
Credit Report	$15
Inspection	$400
Underwriting	$400
Processing	$400
Points	One percent of the loan amount
Origination	One percent of the loan amount
Tax Service	$70
Document Prep	$200
Escrow/Closing	$200
Title Insurance	$500
Recording	$85
Tax Stamps	One percent of the loan amount
Survey/Abstract	$350
Funding Fee	Two percent of the loan amount

That's a lot of fees. Nonrecurring charges are items that must be paid at the time of your closing, and you can't roll them into your loan amount in a purchase loan (with the exception of your funding fee), except when you refinance your mortgage.

But guess what? Most of these charges are regulated by the VA, and therefore they are only allowed to charge you for:

- Appraisal/NOV
- Credit Report
- Title Insurance and Title-Related Charges
- Origination and Discount Point(s)
- Recording
- Survey or Abstract

One easy way to remember which fees you're allowed to pay is to remember the acronym ACTORS: Appraisal (NOV), Credit, Title, Origination (and discount points), Recording, Survey (or abstract). There. That's it.

One important note: If standard loan charges are not allowed to be charged to the veteran, yet they still must be paid, who pays for them? The seller can, the lender can, you can, or any combination thereof.

Wait a second. How can the veteran pay nonallowable closing costs if the VA forbids it? A recent change in VA lending has been the lender "one percent" guideline.

Lenders can have various fees and costs associated with their loan department show up on most loans. Common examples are document preparation charges, lock-in fees, processing or underwriting fees, tax service fees, application fees, and the appraisal. But, in lieu of the borrower paying these fees individually, the lender is allowed to charge a flat one percent of the loan amount and apply that fee to the various miscellaneous lender charges the veteran may not otherwise pay for. For almost anything that is usual or customary for that lender to charge, the veteran can elect to pay the one percent charge and have all those fees taken care of.

This method of using your VA entitlement to get a no-money-down loan and also pay no closing costs is sometimes called a "VA No-No," although I haven't heard that term used much lately. But if you hear that expression from your Realtor or loan officer, you'll know what they're talking about.

Another way to have those nonallowable charges paid for is to have the seller of the property pay them for you, and this is perhaps the most common method. VA loans are unique in this regard; the seller can contribute up to 4 percent of the sales price to your closing costs. (The actual percentage is something your Realtor will help you determine.)

What if the seller says "no" and declines your offer to have them pay your allowable and nonallowable charges? Change your offer and increase the sales price by the amount of the closing fees you wish the seller to pay.

For example, your allowable closing charges might be $3,000, your nonallowables are $3,000, and the home you want to buy is $200,000. First, say outright, "Here's my offer of $200,000—and please pay $6,000 of my closing costs."

If the seller says "yes," then you win. If he says "no," simply offer $206,000 for the home and again ask him to pay $6,000 of your fees. In reality, the seller won't just say "no" and move on, but will instead make a counteroffer. For example, the seller may say, "No, but I'll pay $3,000 of your closing costs instead of $6,000." At that point, take a look at the counteroffer and determine if it's something you want to do. If it's not what you want, take the $3,000 and increase your offer by the other $3,000.

Either way, the seller comes away with the same amount of money at the settlement table, and you just moved some pieces of the puzzle around to get your desired result. But doesn't that increase your mortgage payment if you added another $3,000 or $6,000?

Sure, but really not by much. On a $200,000 loan, 6.50 percent at thirty years is $1,257. A loan amount of $203,000 under those same terms yields a $1,276 payment, or a difference of only $19. Yes, that's higher, but not by much. And certainly easier than pulling money out of savings accounts you may not have or wish to use for something else.

Seller-paid closing fees are an efficient way to handle your costs at closing.

Having Your Lender Pay for Closing Costs

Another way to pay for these costs is to have the lender pay for them. Yes, your lender.

Remember that a discount point of one percent typically reduces your interest rate by one-quarter of a percent. Conversely, increasing your interest rate by one-quarter of percent also nets one percent of your loan amount, which is a credit that can be applied to your closing costs.

Let's say that the seller says "no" and declines to pay for your closing fees, or maybe you decide not to increase the sales price of the home. Instead of a 6.50 percent rate, your rate would go up to 6.75

percent and you would get a $2,000 closing-cost credit from your lender or mortgage broker.

Again, you've increased your liability but you didn't write a check for closing costs. Your monthly payment on 6.75 percent goes up by $32 to $1,289. Your lender will issue a credit at your closing, but in the end, it is you who pay for those closing costs in the form of a higher monthly payment. Not a lot higher, but higher nonetheless.

Consider this option carefully. Even though your monthly payment isn't going to be that much higher when the lender pays for your closing fees, it can add up over the years. If you own that property for more than five years, you'll "break even" with the closing-cost subsidy from the lender, and from that point forward that higher monthly payment is no longer subsidized by the lender's generosity.

At $32 per month, in month 63, or just over five years, that adds up to $2,000, the very same amount the lender credited you. Yet, if you simply don't have the cash to pay for your closing fees and the seller won't pay them, then you don't have much choice.

Others may argue to go ahead and take the higher monthly payment, then invest that $2,000 you would otherwise have paid in points, and after five years and at 8 percent annual return that $2,000 will be equal to about $2,900. That's true, you can invest your money in an account to get a particular yield, but you really need to ask yourself if that's what you'll do. If the answer is "definitely," then this is a good strategy for you. If you're not sure, then consider paying your closing costs out of pocket if you can.

Of course, another way to pay your closing costs is through the lender's one percent offering. On a $200,000 loan, that's $2,000 that can go toward your closing costs. The closing costs as calculated by your lender, that is; there could be additional closing fees that are usual and customary for your area that don't belong to your lender, such as title insurance or closing fees.

This method is really an advantage the larger your loan amount is. Why? Because most closing costs are fixed items and not a percentage of your loan amount. Your appraisal will cost about $350 regardless of how big your loan is, for example.

Yet one percent of $75,000 is much lower than one percent of $400,000, right? That means the lower loan amount would get you a

$750 credit while the $400,000 loan would give you a $4,000 benefit. The appraisal alone on the $75,000 sales price would eat up nearly half of that one percent lender charge, whereas with a $400,000 loan, you'd still have $3,650 left to apply somewhere else, after the appraisal charge.

The final option is a combination of any of the above methods. If you have $4,000 of closing costs, you could have the seller pay $2,000, then increase your rate by one-quarter of a percent to get another $2,000 credit on a $200,000 deal. Or you could get a one percent lender charge and have the seller pay the rest, and so on.

What if none of them work? What if no one is willing to contribute to your closing fees or pay for nonallowables? If you aren't allowed to pay certain types of closing fees and the seller can't pay them and you don't want to, and if you don't want your rate to go up, it might be a situation that you simply can't close your deal the way you wanted to close it.

In this case, your lender may be forced into paying for your nonallowables, and not by charging you one percent.

When lenders first begin quoting VA rates and fees to you, you will find that they are quoting against one another. Loan officer A is trying her best to give you her best deal, and Loan officer B at another lender is also competing.

There's not a whole lot to compete with on a VA loan, other than your rate and the allowable closing costs. Still, you want your loan officers to be aware that they're competing with other lenders. Sometimes when loan officers compete for your loan, they'll start doing everything they can to get your deal . . . even by making less money.

There's no set rule on how much a loan officer is supposed to quote you. Although certain lenders may have minimum amounts the loan officer needs to collect on each loan, other loan companies have no minimum, or if they do it's not much.

Loan officers usually get paid by splitting the income derived from your loan. If you pay $2,000 in points, then the loan officer would split that $2,000 with her mortgage company. To get your loan in-house, you might see one loan officer begin to shed some potential profit. So you're likely to run into a loan officer who is not only willing to pay for your nonallowables, but at the same time won't increase your rate to make up for that subsidy. He's taking it out of the fees he would normally charge you. Instead of the loan officer splitting $2,000, she might pay for $1,000 of your closing costs then split the remaining $1,000 with her company.

Reading the Good Faith Estimate

Federal lending laws require that a loan officer tell you what your estimated closing costs will be. This is called the "good faith estimate" and it is just that: an estimate made to you in all good faith.

The loan officer is required to complete this form, provide it to you, and keep a copy of it in the file. You need to review it, sign it, then mail or fax it back to the loan officer.

When you are face-to-face with a loan officer making an application, that loan officer is required to give you an estimate then and there. If you are applying online or using another method where you're not sitting in front of your loan officer, laws require the loan officer to send you the good faith estimate within three business days of receiving your application.

This is where it can get dicey if you don't know what to watch out for. Loan officers want to try and appear to have the best overall mortgage proposal so they can mix up your good faith estimate by lowballing certain fees at the time of your loan application.

Take this advice to heart: Loan officers have control of their fees only and don't control other third-party charges such as attorney, title, insurance, or any other nonlender or mortgage broker fees.

One way loan officers can appear to be better is when they quote nonlender charges. Let's say an attorney fee is usually $200 and the survey is $400, but the loan officer only quotes $100 for the attorney and $200 for the surveyor. Once you review the good faith estimate, that loan officer's deal will appear to be better than another loan officer's due to the lower fees.

But nonlender charges don't change from one lender to the next. Just getting a lowball quote from a loan officer doesn't mean the attorney must charge the lower fee. Heck no, the attorney will charge what she normally charges, regardless of what the loan officer quoted.

For instance, when you are searching for the best rate, you must also get a quote on the closing costs those lenders are charging. After all, if Lender A quotes you 6.00 percent and Lender B wants 6.25 percent, it might appear to be a no-brainer, no?

Actually, no.

What if Lender A, who had the lowest rate, also charged two discount points and an origination fee for that 6 percent, while Lender B only asked for a one percent origination fee?

For a $400,000 loan, the monthly payment at 6 percent is $2,386 and at 6.25 percent it is $2,450. That's a $64 per month difference, yet you had to pay an additional two discount points to Lender A for that lower payment . . . or $8,000.

It makes no sense to pay $8,000 for a $64 per month savings. You have to look at the fine print and compare not just the rate but also the fees associated with that rate to get a true picture of your best deal.

That's what the good faith estimate is supposed to do: give you a true comparison among two or three lenders' rate offerings. A good faith estimate would show you that Lender A wasn't a good deal after all.

Loan officers can manipulate the good faith estimate and often do because they want to get your deal in the door. Loan officers are required to present an honest proposal, and there are guidelines to follow to make sure what you were originally quoted matches up with the rate and fee structure you find at your settlement. Normally, this variance is about one-eighth of a percent.

In reality, closing costs disclosed at the closing table may be different from what was originally quoted to you. And there is nothing you can do, except call the loan officer and complain or walk away from the table completely, possibly putting your earnest money and your property in jeopardy.

When you are caught up in your zeal to find the best deal, stop to remember this: It's not just the rates; it's the fees, too.

There are experiments in the closing cost game that have met some resistance but actually make a lot of sense. These cost estimates are called "one fee" estimates, where the lender or loan officer simply quotes you one charge—say, $3,500—and everything is paid for. No

$100 difference here or $50 there; it's all right there in black-and-white. You'll know exactly what your fees are.

This closing cost experiment has been trying to break through for a few years now with little success, primarily because lending guidelines and government requirements have yet to make allowances for the one-fee concept.

Another major bank has introduced a "no lender fee" loan that waives typical lender charges such as underwriting fees or document preparation charges. But it's hard to verify if lenders are waiving those fees or, in reality, increasing their overall interest rates to cover those charges.

The easiest way to compare closing costs from one lender or mortgage broker to another is to completely disregard nonlender fees. They will be what they will be, correct? Your insurance policy rate is determined by the insurance agent, not the lender. So although you certainly want to review those fees, don't pay any attention to them when you're still deciding on a lender.

Instead, focus on the lender fees. These charges are found at the very top of your good faith estimate on the line items that start with the number 800, 801, 802, and so on. This section is labeled "Items Payable in Connection with Loan" and they are the fees the lender can have control over.

By isolating just the lender fees, you'll overcome the biggest obstacle in getting a fair as well as firm rate quote.

Negotiating Fees

You can negotiate certain fees . . . but you can only negotiate a fee with the person or company charging the fee and not the person who merely quotes it. And most typically those fees will be associated with your VA lender, and they are the ones you're allowed to pay.

Your appraisal fee is typically something that's not negotiable. Your credit report is something the lender orders but you pay for. Title charges can vary by state, and some states let title companies compete with one another on price. Other states regulate title insurance charges.

Origination and discount points are a function of your rate, yet you have control over the fee quoted to you. As a veteran or qualified VA borrower, you can't pay more than two discount points and one percent origination fee from the lender. Recording fees are usually set in stone.

You don't have to be charged a full percentage point. It can be no points, or one-half point, or even a flat fee of $1,000, or whatever. You can negotiate with your loan officer from one point to seven-eighths of a point, for instance. Or you can say, "Reduce my point by one-eighth and pay for my appraisal and credit report."

What you're doing when negotiating fees is eating away at the loan officer's commission check. But don't think that you'll automatically get whatever you ask for. Although you can certainly negotiate with your loan officer, the loan officer is also negotiating with you . . . and determining whether it's worth it to work with you. If your loan officer likes to make a couple of thousand dollars on each loan and your loan is only bringing in a few hundred bucks, she may not be all that inclined on working with you.

There's a lot of work going on when finding and closing a mortgage loan, and no one can work for free . . . at least not for very long. That doesn't mean you shouldn't ask for discounts or reduced rates. You won't get one if you don't ask for one.

As you seek to negotiate your closing costs, understand that it's not a given that fees will be reduced. Just because a fee is there doesn't mean that it can be reduced. After all, those people or companies providing those services have to make a profit as well or they won't be in business very long, either.

If you receive a good faith estimate that's way off, say, much higher or much lower than what you've received from other loan officers, you need to find out why. Sometimes, the loan officer is either new to the business or not familiar with working with VA loans. If you get a good faith estimate that has nonallowable charges listed or doesn't include the funding fee, then you're probably getting a VA quote from someone who is more likely to drop the ball during your closing.

If you read a good faith estimate and there are charges that shouldn't be there and you call your loan officer and he says something like, "Oh, don't worry about it, it's just an estimate," either the loan officer didn't know how to prepare a VA good faith or he paid little attention to the fact that you were getting a VA loan and quoted you a conventional loan. Either way, you want to avoid working with that person. A good faith is a good way to see if loan officers were telling the truth when they told you they were familiar with VA loans.

The very last VA loan closing cost fee is the funding fee. And it's on every single VA loan issued, and it is nonnegotiable. The funding fee is a required fee that helps to fund the VA guaranty. If a loan goes south, it's the proceeds from the funding fee that help to offset any losses. The standard funding fee is 2.15 percent of the loan amount for those who use their VA entitlement for the first time.

Funding fees can also be rolled into the new loan amount, for purchase or refinance loans, as long as the loan amount does not exceed the current VA maximum loan. The funding fee can also vary depending on the veteran's type of service and whether the veteran put any money into the transaction as a down payment, as shown in Figure 6–1.

Figure 6–1. Funding fee table.

	Amount Down	First Time	Second Time
Regular Military	0%	2.15%	3.3%
	5%–10%	1.50%	1.50%
	10%+	1.25%	1.25%
Eligible Reserves/	0%	2.40%	3.3%
National Guard	5%–10%	1.75%	1.75%
	10%+	1.50%	1.50%

There are exemptions from the funding fee altogether, and they are reserved for those veterans receiving service-related disability pay and for surviving spouses of veterans who died in combat or from a service-related injury.

Other changes in the funding fee are reserved for cash-out refinances and Interest Rate Reduction Loans (discussed in Chapter 7). Funding fees will change based on the amount of the loan compared to the sales price, too. But every VA loan requires a funding fee in most every case.

It's not a requirement that you roll your funding fee into your loan amount. You may choose to pay for it in cash, or you may roll part of it in the loan amount and cover the rest with your own funds, with funds from the seller, or from a lender subsidy.

Typically, when you put some money down on a mortgage loan, a VA loan may not be your best choice because of the funding fee. If you have 5 percent or 10 percent down or more, then there are other options besides a VA loan that do not require the funding fee. We'll discuss those loan options in more detail in Chapter 8.

CHAPTER 7

Refinancing, Equity Lending, and Special VA Programs

So far we've covered the basic VA purchase. In this chapter, we'll discuss additional loan programs available to qualified veterans and active duty personnel. We've looked at fixed- and adjustable-rate loans, and glanced at a few others. Now, let's look at the few others in more detail.

Refinancing a VA Loan

A refinance mortgage is lending terminology for simply "doing the same loan all over again." You may not have to keep the same lender, but you're keeping the property, just changing the terms of your current loan.

But, in addition to redoing your current mortgage, you might also want to pull out some equity from your home or maybe use some money to make home improvements, such as adding a deck, an extra room, or even a second story.

Officially, refinancing is the act of replacing one mortgage loan with another. The VA, however, has a special term for refinancing, called an Interest Rate Reduction Loan, or IRRL.

The IRRL is unique to VA loans. Yes, every loan on the planet has the ability to be refinanced, yet the VA is special because no matter what has happened, creditwise, since the VA loan was originally issued, the veteran automatically qualifies for the new loan if it can be shown that the loan will reduce the veteran's total monthly payments.

Normally, a refinance loan is just like a purchase loan in that the applicant must qualify all over again. It might seem silly at first to have to qualify once more for a refinance loan; after all, if you can handle the monthly payments at 7.50 percent, then you should be able to swing 6.50 percent.

Still, lenders ask that you qualify all over again. Yet, with the IRRL, debt ratios and credit are less of a concern if the rate is being reduced . . . if it is, hello, IRRL.

This is a huge advantage for a VA loan. Often, people who buy a house find their circumstances have changed for the worse. Perhaps someone got laid off, got sick, or got a divorce. Earnings and credit can change. But that is of little consequence with a VA loan.

Usually people refinance because interest rates have dropped and the homeowner wants to take advantage of lower monthly payments. There are other reasons to refinance a mortgage loan, but usually it's because rates have gone down. There is a lot of clutter regarding when to refinance and when not to.

There is an urban myth that it's not worth refinancing unless mortgage rates have dropped at least 2 percent below your current rate. This generalization stems from the fact that there are closing costs involved in a refinance just as there are with a purchase. But that's hogwash.

Specifically, it makes sense to refinance if you own the property long enough to recover the closing costs associated with the new loan.

How much are closing costs in a refinance? They're almost identical to the closing costs of an original purchase, with perhaps the biggest exception being title insurance charges. Because title insurance insures against previous claims and fraud, not much should have changed from when you bought the property. In practice, title insurance will insure the time from when you bought the house to the time you're refinancing . . . typically just a couple of years in certain markets.

When considering a refinance, first consider the available interest rates. If they have gone down, then consider your closing charges.

Another benefit of VA loans is that the IRRL is "streamlined." In fact, it is often called a VA Streamline, or *streamline refinance*. The veteran does not have to pay for an appraisal, because no appraisal is needed. Nor is there a credit check. Nor are debt ratios calculated.

For the remaining costs associated with a refinance, the veteran can increase the rate to cover the other charges, roll those fees into the new loan amount, or any combination thereof.

What's a good drop in rate before a refinance should be considered? In reality, that depends perhaps as much on the loan size as the rate. A one percent difference in rate can mean a lot more in terms of monthly payment when comparing $400,000 and $50,000 loan amounts.

For example, 7 percent on a thirty-year $400,000 mortgage is $2,645 per year. If rates drop one percent to 6 percent, the resulting payment goes to $2,386 . . . a difference of $259 per month. That's a lot.

Using those same rates, on a $50,000 loan, the payments are $331 and $298, respectively . . . a difference of $33. Remember that fixed costs in mortgage loans are immune to the effects of loan amounts. That is, just the appraisal charge alone of $350 would take nearly a year (ten months) to recover. Not to mention the other charges of title insurance and closing charges. A list of standard closing costs would look like this:

Standard Closing Costs

Notice of Value (NOV)	$350
Credit	$15
Closing/Escrow	$200
Title Insurance	$500
Recording	$85
Total	$1,465

To determine if a refinance is in your best interest, divide the monthly savings into the closing costs. In this example, divide $259 into the $1,465 and you get almost six months. But if you took the same approach to the smaller loan amount of $50,000, you'll see that it takes just over forty-four months, or almost four years, to recover those same fees.

These are only rough closing cost estimates, as fees will vary depending upon your location, but what's most important is the method for how to determine when it's a good idea to consider refinancing. This example also points to another suggestion that I make, and that is to rarely, if ever, pay discount points or origination charges with any mortgage loan. That way, if rates go down enough that you want to refinance, and you didn't pay points on the previous loan, you won't have "lost" the discounted rate.

For instance, let's say you bought your house two years ago for $250,000 and had a choice between 6.50 percent at no points or 6.25 percent at one point. The difference in monthly payments is about $40 per month. But you chose to pay the point to get the lower rate, meaning you paid another $2,500 for the lower payment. That means it would take $2,500 / $40 = 62.5 months to recover that "point."

Because rates were at relative lows, you decided to buy down that mortgage by another one-quarter percent. Rates couldn't go any lower. Or so you thought.

Yet rates did drop. They dropped to 5.75 percent, and you're thinking of refinancing that once-low 6.25 percent rate. But you now have to consider the fact that you "lost" $1,540 in the discount point you originally paid. That means you never made it to the sixty-two month recovery milestone.

It still makes sense to refinance in this example, but you essentially lost $1,540. I'm a big fan of keeping acquisition costs low, and that means taking a hard look at paying points or origination fees.

One word of caution at this stage: You will hear loan officers either advertise or tell you straight out that they can refinance your VA loan while you skip two payments. Sounds like a pretty good deal, doesn't it? If you hear loan officers or lenders make this pitch, find someone else . . . they're trying to mislead you and they're doing it intentionally.

Remember that interest is paid in arrears. Each day of the month, your per diem interest is added to your loan balance, and when you make your next mortgage payment it will include the interest accrued from the previous month.

When you refinance, your loan processor will order a payoff from your current VA lender and specify a closing date. A payoff is the current principal balance plus accrued interest. Your current lender will send your processor the payoff amount.

If your loan balance is $150,000 and your interest payment is $31.43 per day, and you're closing on the fifteenth of the month, the payoff would be $150,000 plus fifteen days at $31.43 per day, or $150,000 + $471 = $150,471.

And just like when you bought your home, the new lender will collect prepaid interest up to the first of the following month. If you closed on the fifteenth, then the new lender would collect fifteen days of interest to the first of the next month at a new lower rate, say, $29.82 per day. Fifteen days of that per diem rate is $447, plus your old payoff amount of $150,471 equals $150,918. Usually this interest is simply added to your loan amount at closing. Although it will feel as if you didn't make your next month's payment, you really did—$447 of it—but you added it to your loan amount and didn't have to write a separate check for it.

A loan officer could tell you not to write this month's mortgage payment or next month's mortgage payment because she'll take care of it in the refinance and you'll simply skip them. But you didn't skip them; you borrowed them and put them in your loan amount.

All loan officers know how this payoff is calculated; they're just trying to make it sound as if they have the better deal.

One more piece of advice: When someone tells you not to make your mortgage payment, take heed and make it anyway. If your mortgage payment falls beyond the fifteenth of the month (in this example), you'll get hit with a penalty.

Something could happen during the course of your refinance application. Rates could change and you wait a bit longer, or you decide to move on to another lender, or you simply change your mind and decide not to do anything.

If you wait to pay, you could run the risk of a late payment with your current mortgage lender. If you do decide to wait and pay off your old mortgage to "skip" a monthly payment, understand that there are risks involved with not paying on time.

Another reason to refinance, other than to reduce the monthly payment, is to change the term. You might want to refinance from a fifteen-year to a thirty-year loan, or the other way around. The difference in monthly payment between a fifteen-year and thirty-year loan can be considerable. A fifteen-year loan at 5.50 percent on $300,000 is $2,440, but a thirty-year loan at 6.00 percent is $1,789. That's $650 per month difference.

Sometimes homeowners want to reduce monthly payments, and they can do that by switching loan terms. Perhaps there's been a job loss or some other event where lower monthly payments are necessary. In this case, simply changing the term will reduce the payment.

On the other hand, sometimes people refinance out of a thirty-year loan and into a fifteen-year loan. The monthly payments might change, yet the difference in interest saved is striking. At $300,000, a fifteen-year rate of 5.50 percent yields nearly $140,000 in interest paid to the lender, extended to full term. Similarly, a thirty-year loan at 5.50 percent results in over $300,000 in interest paid to the lender. That's huge.

I recall a refinance that I did for a guy a few years ago who had a different reason to refinance: He wanted to be mortgage-free when his daughter was old enough to go to college . . . exactly fifteen years from the date he refinanced.

Another reason to refinance is to change from an adjustable-rate mortgage (ARM) to a fixed rate. If you have an ARM and fixed rates are headed downward or are, better yet, lower than your ARM, it's a good time to get out of an adjustable rate.

Let's say your ARM, based on a one-year Treasury index plus a margin of 2.50 percent, is fully indexed at 7.50 percent and fixed rates are at 6.00 percent. Do you think it's a good idea to get out of the ARM and into a fixed? I do. Is it a good idea to get out of an ARM and into a fixed rate if your ARM was at 7.50 percent and the fixed was at 6.75 percent?

It depends on how long it would take to recover the closing costs associated with the refinance compared with how long you intend to keep that same mortgage.

Okay, trick question: Would it make sense to refinance out of an ARM if your fully indexed rate was at 7 percent and fixed rates were at 7 percent? Should you refinance out of an ARM into a fixed if the fixed rate were even a little higher?

It might make sense. Even if the fixed note is a little higher. Now you're wondering: How can that be?

If you've got an adjustable-rate mortgage, your one-year Treasury index is sitting at 5 percent, your margin is at 2.50 percent, and rates are continuing to move up, you might be held "artificially low" due to your interest rate cap.

Your fully indexed rate might want to go 8 percent, but it can't because of the cap. If, during the coming year, the one-year Treasury hit 5.50 percent, then your rate next year would go to 8 percent, when you could have locked in a fixed rate at 7 percent.

Folks, interest rates were in the high teens in the early 1980s. It could happen again. It's not likely, but it could.

If you have an adjustable-rate mortgage and mortgage rates are at relative lows, then you can make a strong case for refinancing into a fixed mortgage—if for no other reason than to sleep at night without worrying about what your house payment might be three years from now.

Should You Take Out Equity?

Pulling cash out of a property's equity is another reason to refinance. Before I explain, let me note one important exception: Once cash is pulled from a property, it no longer qualifies as a VA Streamline. A streamline only applies when either just the rate or the term is adjusted and no money is pulled out of the home.

Now, let's say your property is valued at $500,000 and you owe $200,000. You can both refinance the current rate to a lower one or change the term to fit your requirements and also walk away from the settlement table with some money in your pocket. How much? Depending upon where you live, you could borrow up to 90 percent of the value of your home. Typically, though, the maximum is at 80 percent of the value, primarily because your rate will be higher if you choose to get 90 percent of the value instead of 80 percent.

Maybe you don't want all of it; maybe you just want to get a lower rate and pull out, say, $75,000. You can do mostly whatever you want with that $75,000. Perhaps you want to pay off an automobile loan or a credit card or two. Maybe you want to add a deck to your home. Heck, maybe you just want to take a really, really nice vacation. When you refinance a mortgage and pull money out at the same time, it's called a *cash-out refinance.*

With a cash-out refinance, you'll encounter the standard VA allowable closing costs, so you'll either need to pay for them by taking a higher rate or deducting those closing costs from the proceeds of the loan.

Please understand what's happening here, because you'll be asked by loan officers or hear advertisements exhorting you to "pull cash out of your home and pay bills" or whatever. In fact, a loan officer will make a pretty good case to pull money out of your home to pay off credit card bills. However, interest rates on credit cards and automobile loans will be lower than what your mortgage rate will be. The math always works, from a month-to-month basis, that is.

If your car payment is $500 per month and the loan balance is $30,000, then the loan officer will look at your loan application and say something like, "You know, if you pulled $30,000 out of your home and paid off your car, it would drop your monthly payment by over $300 per month. That's a heck of a savings."

And he would be right, although it would be on a month-to-month savings. If you put that $30,000 automobile loan into your mortgage and amortized it over thirty years, you would have paid an additional $24,000 in interest. Interest you would not have otherwise paid.

A similar review can be made when a loan officer talks to you about paying off credit card balances with mortgage loans. Remember, all this is done in the guise of lowering your monthly payments and replacing those monthly payments with tax-deductible ones: mortgage interest.

The drawback with paying off credit cards is that if you charge those cards back up again with that same high rate, you've replaced your shorter-term debt with a long-term debt, adding more to your interest payments. If you only pay minimums on your credit cards each month and look into doing a cash-out refinance to pay off those high-interest-rate cards, make sure you don't rack up a lot of new charges on those cards again. That could spell trouble down the road.

Cash-out refinancing can be done for other reasons, but perhaps one of the most profitable, from a homeowner's perspective, is for home improvements. Borrowing money at lower rates and reducing your monthly payments while also increasing the value of your property is a very attractive proposition.

For example, let's review a scenario where a homeowner refinances to a lower rate and uses those funds to improve the home:

Current Loan Balance	$200,000
Current Value	$400,000
Current Mortgage Rate	7.00%
Monthly Payment	$1,299
New Kitchen and Deck	$100,000
New Cash-Out Loan	$300,000
New Mortgage Rate	6.00%
New Monthly Payment	$1,761
New Value of Home	$490,000

You've just increased the value of your home by nearly 25 percent while your monthly payments increased by about $460. So, if interest rates have gone down and you're considering a streamline, also consider options to use your equity in your home for other ways and do a cash-out refinance.

If you decide to use those funds for a remodel, you're getting most of your investment back in the form of increased value.

Should You Refinance into a VA Loan?

Here's an important piece of the refinance equation that needs to be discussed: It's not always in your best interest to take a VA loan. (We'll look at that issue in more detail in Chapter 8.) If you've got equity in your home that you've realized in one form or the other—by appreciation, standard amortization, or simply paying ahead on your mortgage—you might want to consider other loan alternatives. Specifically, loans that don't require you to pay a funding fee when you refinance. If you'll recall from the funding fee table in Chapter 6 (see Figure 6–1), these fees can be 3 percent or more of your loan amount.

In other words . . . you'll want to look at a conventional loan if you're gaining equity in your property.

Another way to pull equity out of your home is to use an *equity loan,* sometimes called an equity line of credit. It's not a VA loan, but it can be used in conjunction with one.

Equity Line of Credit

An equity loan is a second mortgage (usually) that rests behind any first mortgage and is low in cost, yet slightly higher in rate. So, if you wanted $100,000 for home improvements, you would apply for a second mortgage, the equity loan, with a rate typically about 2 percent higher than similar fixed mortgages for first notes, or a loan based on the prime rate plus one or two percent.

These loans are sometimes called a home equity line of credit, or HELOC.

A $100,000 equity loan at 8.50 percent amortized over thirty years would give you a $764 monthly payment, which is much higher than a cash-out refinance. However, mortgage rates aren't always low when you want them to be, and you want to add a deck and remodel your kitchen now and not wait.

At first glance, you say, "Whoa, that's a lot," and it may be. But it's also a lot less expensive to acquire. Second mortgages carry few closing costs, usually only a couple of hundred bucks or so. In fact, many lenders even waive that fee if you ask them hard enough.

That's an equity loan. An *equity line* is a line of credit that, again, is based on the value of your home. It's similar to having a checking account with your balance being home equity. In fact, an equity line does give you a checkbook. When you need or want money, you simply write a check for it and you'll get a statement the following month asking for a payment.

You don't pay interest on an equity line until you actually draw on it, and you can pay off the balance any time you want, using the line over and over again. Equity lines are also cheap, most often free.

Both an equity loan and an equity line won't go above certain limits. These limits are based upon the value of the home compared to all loans/lines placed against it.

For instance, if your home is valued at $300,000 and your current balance is $200,000, then your loan-to-value ratio, or LTV, is:

$$\$200,000 / \$300,000 = .6667, \text{ or } 67 \text{ LTV}$$

Now, add a $50,000 equity line of credit. That new $50,000 HELOC plus the $200,000 current mortgage comes to $250,000. Divide that by $300,000 and the number is 83.33. This is a combined loan to value, or CLTV, of 83.

Shopping for a Refinance

You can get refinance loans at any place that offers VA loans. And you need to shop that refinance rate just as hard as you did when you bought the house. It's the very same drill . . . decide on your loan program, get referrals, then start making phone calls.

One advantage of refinancing, as compared to getting a loan for purchasing a home, is that you're not constrained by time. At least from a contract standpoint. When you bought the property, your sales contract told you when you were going to close. Most often with thirty days. You would have that thirty day period to find a lender and lock in your rate. But with a refinance, you don't have that time constraint any longer. You can wait to refinance until the cows come home. Or longer.

Still, you need to prepare ahead of time if you think a refinance might be in your near future. Don't wait until you read in the newspaper that interest rates hit record lows, then start your loan application to refinance right now. Instead, always be aware of what rates are doing . . . or better yet, in addition, have your loan officer contact you when she thinks it might be getting close to considering a refinance.

I routinely research my database of clients and look for people who just might be candidates for refinancing should rates move just a tad more. Then, when their target rate does hit, they're ready to go and can close within a few days . . . getting the absolute best rate available.

That's a unique advantage with a refinance mortgage; you can work it until the time is just right . . . your time. But don't get greedy.

No one, I mean *no one*, knows where mortgage rates are headed. Sure, there may be some short-term speculation about what might happen to rates in the next quarter, but no one knows what's going to happen over the next year. But you should be aware of how rates are moving. Many times, you won't have to pay much attention at all; instead, you'll be hit over the head with radio or newspaper advertisements saying, "Rates are low. Refinance now!"

Find your selected lender, make an application, supply the requested paperwork (yes, you'll still need your Certificate of Eligibility again), and wait. Be wary, though, because if you did your homework and selected your loan officer, you'll most likely get phone calls from those loan officers who didn't win your deal. They'll call you and say, "Hey, David, we're having a special on VA loans right now, blah, blah, blah . . ."

There can't be that much difference between one VA lender and the other. Make your decision and stick to your guns.

Should You Lock?

If you've gotten to this stage and you've already decided a refinance is a good choice for you, then the next thing you need to decide is "when to lock."

I have been asked this question probably over a thousand times: "Hey David, what do you think rates are going to do?" That really means, "Should I lock right now or wait a few days?"

If I told you to lock today and rates move still lower tomorrow, you'd be mad at me. Or if you wanted to lock today but didn't on my advice and rates moved up, you'd be mad at me even more.

So, what's my magical answer that works every time? It's this:

> I don't know what rates are going to do, but my advice is that whatever you decide to do, assume you make the wrong decision. Which way would you rather be wrong?

I made that up way back in 1992, during the first real refinance boom that I was ever involved with. How does that advice apply to you?

Let's say your decision is wrong. You decided to float and rates moved up, or you decided to lock and rates went down. It's more prudent to be wrong if you decided to lock and rates went down.

On closer examination, greed takes hold. If you're at 6.50 percent and rates move down to 6.00 percent, then you're thinking about refinancing. You select your VA lender, make application, then follow the markets.

Your loan amount is $200,000 and your current monthly payment is $1,237; the new rate at 6 percent results in a new payment of $1,193. You've already done your homework, run the numbers, and have come to the conclusion that the 6 percent rate is a great deal.

But what if rates go even lower? What if they go to 5.875 percent? Or 5.75 percent? Perhaps you decide to wait and you call me and say, "Hey, David, what are rates gonna do?"

I say, "I don't know and nobody does. But I suggest you think about your decision and assume that you make the wrong decision . . . which way would you rather be wrong? Lock now and rates move down further still, or you have a rate you like and rates move up?"

If you follow my advice, you'd lock in. You have already determined that 6 percent is a good deal . . . now all you're looking for is another one-eighth percent. What is one-eighth of a percent on a $200,000 loan? It's $1,183. A difference of about ten bucks compared to the 6 percent rate.

Okay, so you locked in at 6.00 percent and rates went down to 5.875 percent. So what? You still win.

On the other hand, if you got greedy and rates moved up, you lost what you had already thought was acceptable. And guess what else . . . rates shoot upward but inch downward. It takes a lot, *a lot* for rates to go down. But someone can sneeze "inflation" or some Fed Board governor can make the wrong comment at the wrong time and you could lose everything you gained over the previous twelve months.

Mortgage bond traders, like all bond traders, are conservative in this investment. They don't like surprises. They can get spooked easily. That's why mortgage rates, tied to their GNMA (Government National Mortgage Association) bond, can spike yet it takes a Herculean effort to get them to go lower.

Here's how you can get hurt "waiting" for lower rates.

Let's say your new monthly payment would be $1,164, saving you $73. But you think rates are going to move down further still. Based upon all your research of course. So you wait another week or two. Then a month. You think rates are moving down more but they don't.

In fact, they move up to where it doesn't make as much sense to refinance at all. So you wait some more. Then rates begin to move down again and you watch them inch down. Slowly. You lose sleep at night. Then another month goes by. You keep waiting for that magical 5.875 percent rate that never appears, trying to get that additional $15.

Yet you're into month three and 5.875 percent has never arrived.

At this stage, if rates haven't gotten to your magic number, it's possible they never will. But you wait another month, convinced that all the economic reports point to lower rates. Finally, six months go by and you give up.

Rates move back to 6.00 percent. You lock. And after six months you've lost that $73 per month savings by refinancing from 6.50 percent to 6 percent. You lost $438 by waiting. All trying to get an additional $15. You stayed at the higher rate convinced that you could squeeze out another one-eighth percent, even though you had determined that the 6 percent rate was good.

I have seen this scenario played out so many times by consumers that I can't count them. They were my clients and I still couldn't convince them. Greed set in. Maybe they did too much research on the Internet.

If you've already decided you win at 6 percent, then don't try to win even more at 5.875 percent and possibly lose everything. I know that many of you will disagree with me, and that's fine. Just remember: Assume that whatever decision you make will be the wrong one—and *which way would you rather be wrong?* Ironically, if you answer that question correctly, you will in fact have made the right choice.

Maybe it's me, and it certainly could be, but I don't gamble. And neither should you when it comes to your home loan.

Special VA Loan Programs

Besides all the benefits of VA loans, there are other advantages that are offered and guaranteed by the VA when it comes to home loans. There are programs that retrofit homes for the disabled, special benefits for surviving spouses of veterans, and reduced fees for those on disability.

There is a special program within the VA called the Specially Adapted Housing program, or SAH. It is offered to veterans who have sustained a service-related injury and need assistance in retrofitting a home to accommodate certain needs.

Actually, there are a couple of types of SAH programs, and they both come in the form of grants. The first grant is available for those who are confined to wheelchairs; the other grant is for veterans who have blindness in both eyes with a 5/200 visual acuity or less. This program also makes allowances for the loss of use of both hands.

Because it is a grant, you don't have to pay it back, and it is available for qualifying veterans in amounts up to $50,000 to retrofit a house or dwelling to make it compatible with the veteran's disability. These retrofits can widen doors or install wheelchair-compatible carpet or other wheelchair-accessible accessories such as faucets, light switches, sinks, bathrooms . . . whatever is needed to assist the vet.

This grant program is not automatically approved, and you must contact your regional VA Center or call the Veterans Service Center at 1–800–827–1000. It is the service center that will determine whether you're qualified to receive these grants, based on the VA Rating Decision, but typically there are three basic requirements:

1. It must be medically feasible for you to live in the house; in other words, living there by yourself won't harm you or deny you the medical care you need.

2. The house has to be able to be retrofitted to suit your living needs; in other words, you can live there normally.

3. It must be feasible from a financial standpoint, which means you have to show how you're going to make the payments.

These SAH grants have no time limit, so you don't have to use the money within a certain period of time. It's also possible that your disability hasn't reached a stage where you may qualify, or maybe your disability has progressed to the point where you do qualify.

If you don't qualify now, according to your VA Rating Decision, you can always apply again later if you need to. You can also use more grant money for other things if the SAH grant goes up in the future . . . which it probably will. The kicker with this feature is that you can only use a SAH grant three times, and no more.

If future funds are increased to, say, $75,000 and you've used $50,000, then go back to the VA Service Center and apply for the additional $25,000 grant. For all the things available for eligible veterans, $50,000 may not be enough to do everything you need or want to do with your home.

The $50,000 grant can be used for more than just retrofitting or remodeling an existing home. You can also use those funds to help build yourself a new home, either on land you already own or by applying those funds to acquire both the land and the home construction.

There is a limitation, however, in that the grant cannot exceed 50 percent of the value of the home. This means if you use your entire grant, the improvements can't exceed 50 percent of the cost of the home.

When you adapt a home, there will be some special requirements to make certain that the changes you're making are in line with the requirements for specially adapted housing, such as doorways being at least thirty-six inches wide or hallways being at least forty-eight inches wide, and so on.

Your SAH agent is the person who can help you find an architect, find a builder, and get financing for your purchase or remodel. In fact, don't do it any other way. The SAH folks work on grants every day and have people at their disposal who work with disabled and blind veterans to accommodate their needs.

Your SAH agent will then walk you through the process of obtaining your VA loan and help you determine where best to put your grant dollars at work. This is where the "financial feasibility" comes into play.

In order to obtain an SAH, you'll need to qualify for a VA loan and go through the standard VA qualification standards for the loan, just like any other veteran. Once you get a VA approval to buy the house, then you can also apply for the SAH grant to make the improvements you need to make.

One way to help stretch your grant dollars is to first try and find a home previously owned by someone with a disability who may have had some of the retrofit work already done. You may want to look for homes with wider hallways, easy-to-open sliding glass doors, and other disability-related revisions.

To begin the process, you'll fill out Form 26–4555 and mail it to your nearest regional VA Home Loan Center. (See Appendix A.)

Special Home Loan Programs Issued by Individual States

The different states in the union have their own state-sponsored benefits. Although most state VA benefits can include common things such as tuition assistance, free license plate tags, and hunting licenses, along with medical and other benefits, some states offer home loan programs that are in addition to the typical VA home loan.

Such programs are very, very hard to beat. You need to be VA eligible and have all the paperwork you would normally need to have to get a VA loan from a VA lender, but these states offer rates that are still lower than what you can get from the best VA lender in town.

How low? In many cases, one percent lower—or more. If you live in one of these states, contact the department that oversees home loan programs for veterans to see if you qualify.

I know here in Texas, when I could compete against other VA lenders, I would always quote the rate available from the State of Texas, called the Tex-Vet program, offered through the Texas Veterans Land Board. When I would quote a Tex-Vet rate, no one could compete against me. I was always lower than everyone else, and what's odd is that even many lenders don't know that such state programs exist.

The list here is by no means complete, because some states are actually in the process of putting together their own programs that would provide assistance for remodeling a disabled veteran's home (in addition to the federal SAH grants), along with discounted home loan services. Even if your state isn't listed here, use Appendix A to contact your state office and ask if it offers home loan benefits to VA-eligible residents.

Alaska

The State of Alaska sponsors a loan program through the Alaska Housing Finance Corporation (www.ahfc.state.ak.us), which subsidizes the VA mortgage loan program, providing below-market rates.

California

California has the Cal-Vet program (www.cdva.ca.gov/calvet), which has been around for several years and offers loan programs from zero to 20 percent down. Interest rates are below market and can vary depending upon service.

Kentucky

Kentucky (www.kdva.net) started the process to provide qualifying Kentucky veterans with below-market home loans, but as of this writing the details have not been worked out.

Mississippi

Below-market home loans for qualified Mississippi veterans are issued by the Veterans' Home Purchase Board of the State of Mississippi (www.vhpb.state.ms.us/). Currently, available loans are one to two percent below market rates, and there is a maximum $195,000 sales price requirement.

Oregon

The Oregon Department of Veterans' Affairs (www.oregon.gov/ODVA/loans.shtml) offers home loans below market rate for qualified Oregon veterans, as well as home-improvement loans if the home's first mortgage is an ODVA home loan.

Texas

The Texas Veterans Land Board (www.glo.state.tx.us/vlb/) offers below-market rates for existing construction and for land to qualified Texas veterans.

Surviving Spouses of Deceased Veterans

There are also certain benefits for surviving spouses of deceased veterans. In particular when it comes to home loans, you get the full VA home loan benefits as long as your spouse died in service or from a service-related injury. That means you're entitled to absolutely every VA benefit you've read in this book.

Other family members, such as children of the deceased veteran, are not eligible for home loan benefits, nor are any other relatives.

Most VA home loan benefits to surviving spouses go away if the surviving spouse remarries. Under certain circumstances the surviving spouse may be eligible, especially if the individual is older than fifty-seven. You must also have been married upon the death of the veteran (not divorced) and may not have remarried before the age of fifty seven. If portions of the entitlement were previously used, you are eligible to use those benefits, but no new entitlement will be issued.

In addition, if the surviving spouse and the veteran applied and received a VA loan together, the surviving spouse (nonveteran) may still qualify for the IRRL. This is a huge benefit that can reduce the monthly payment for the surviving spouse on essentially a "nonqualifying" basis with no credit or income check.

CHAPTER 8

When VA Loans Are Not Your Best Choice

There are times when your VA entitlement may not be your best choice for a home loan. For instance, if your VA loan will be higher than allowable limits, you won't be able to use your VA loan. If the maximum VA loan lenders will issue is the conforming loan limit, you're out of luck.

That's okay, there are loans that are competitive in that arena without using your VA entitlement. It's just that if you have zero down and fall underneath the limits . . . the VA is hard to beat. When is it easy to beat? Or when is the VA loan not a good idea?

New Construction

Lenders don't make VA construction loans. Construction loans are a slightly different breed and are drawn out over the course of the construction period, usually six months or more as the house is being built.

It's not that the VA won't guarantee a construction loan; it's just that lenders won't issue them. But that's not to say you can't use your VA loan at all with regard to construction; it just has to be spent in a way that falls outside the construction itself.

Construction loans work differently than permanent mortgages. When you decide to build a home, you must first get building plans and specifications from an architect or builder. Then the builder will look at those building plans and, after a couple of weeks, give you an estimate on how much it would cost to build that home. The builder will add up the costs of the nails, hammers, wood, and labor it will take to build the house as it was planned.

You will take those bids to a construction lender—perhaps your bank, but it doesn't have to be—and get a construction loan.

Most construction loans ask for some equity in the deal at the very beginning. That means you need to put some down payment money in the deal before a bank will issue a construction loan.

That's one of the reasons lenders don't make VA construction loans because they typically require some down payment. There are loans that don't require down payment but will use the lot you're going to build on as equity. If it's your land, that is.

If you don't already own the land, you'll need to find your lot to build on. Getting a land or lot loan (they're the same) usually requires some down payment money as well. If you're going to build and you don't have land to build it on, you'll need to find a place to do so.

There are new loans that will allow you to both acquire the land, build the home, and get your permanent mortgage on it all rolled into one. But it's not a VA loan, and the rates will be higher than what the VA could offer on a regular mortgage.

Let's say you own the land, get a quote to build for $300,000, and you get a construction loan. The bank won't just hand your builder $300,000 and say, "Okay, go build that house."

That could be risky.

Instead, the bank will ask the builder to let it know when certain stages of the construction are completed, then the bank will dole out portions of that $300,000 loan to the builder to reimburse that builder for money he's already spent or invested in the construction project.

As the lot is cleared and your slab is poured, the builder would go to the bank and say, "Hey, I've gotten this far. I need some money." And the bank will send out an inspector to see if in fact the lot was cleared and the slab was poured. If so, the bank issues the builder some money. If the construction is to be built in six phases, the bank will issue one-sixth of $300,000, or $50,000. Then the house would be framed and electrical and plumbing would be installed or the roof would be put on, and so on.

During the course of the construction, money is handed to the builder in predetermined increments until the home is completed 100 percent. At the end of construction, the builder has been paid and you owe $300,000 to the bank, plus interest that has accrued during your construction period.

VA loans aren't like that. Money can't be distributed to a builder in increments with a VA loan.

Now you need a mortgage, sometimes called a *permanent mortgage,* when speaking of construction. Whereas the construction note is temporary, the permanent is just your regular mortgage.

At this stage, you can use your VA loan to replace the construction note. But you can't use it for construction funds. In fact, one of the best ways to negotiate your construction loan and get the best terms—or even get approved, for that matter—is to get your VA approval before you go to the construction lender. This way, the bank knows that no matter what happens during the construction process, even if there may be some past or current credit issues, you have your VA approval from your VA lender. This will help things out tremendously if you're not sure if you can qualify for a construction loan.

There's more risk in a construction loan than a permanent mortgage. If you default during construction or otherwise something bad happens, the bank is sitting on an unfinished house with no buyer and is losing money by the day. But with a solid commitment that you'll replace that construction loan with a VA mortgage already approved . . . well, you can see why it's a huge benefit.

Another time a VA loan can be used in conjunction with construction is with a builder who is building a home that doesn't yet have a buyer. He's building the home and speculating that he'll be able to sell it to a yet-unnamed buyer. This is called a "spec" home.

VA loans will work just like any other loan in this case; when the house is finished, you simply use your VA loan to buy it. It's the spec builder who is putting up his own money (or is borrowing it from a bank) to build the home and sell it for a profit.

When you visit a new subdivision, you'll see all these fancy new homes being built. Brand-new ones. No one has ever lived in them and they are all boasting new appliances, new floors, and new carpet. As a builder moves into a new subdivision, it's likely you'll be buying a house that's not yet built but is being started. Most often in a new development you won't need a construction loan, because the builder has already secured construction funds from his bank and will sell the homes as buyers come to buy them.

You can use your VA loan in this scenario as well. You just can't use your VA loan to build.

A new breed of construction loans is called the *one-time close* loan, where you get construction money plus your permanent mortgage all wrapped into one closing and one note. A one-time close loan lets you know what your permanent mortgage rate will be, six months before you close. Although the rate might not be the absolute best, at least you'll know what it will be.

When you get a construction loan, there will be one set of closing costs. You'll need an appraisal, some title work, and so on. When you replace your construction loan with a permanent one, you'll also have a new set of costs. You'll have two closings.

The appeal of the one-time close loan is that you can save on closing costs because you'll only have one closing, not two. This argument is a bit misleading, though. The implication is that two closings mean double the closing costs, yet in reality those same closing costs are spread out over two loans. There will be some additional charges when you have two loans, but not many.

A one-time close loan shouldn't be decided on based upon saving money on closing costs.

One note of caution: Some construction lenders ask for a "commitment" fee up-front that is usually a one percent origination charge. This is money paid at the very beginning of the construction project, and it is essentially "insurance" that you won't go to another lender for the permanent mortgage. Your construction lender can also be your permanent lender.

If you decide to get two loans—a construction then a permanent— don't be surprised by a commitment fee. If your construction loan is $300,000, then your commitment fee could be $3,000. Nonrefundable. When you go to closing, that $3,000 fee can be applied to your origination or discount point or some other lender charge for a permanent loan, but if you choose to find another permanent lender, then you could lose your $3,000.

Not every lender has such a policy, so do your homework.

During construction, if rates go down and you chose a one-time close, then your VA rate will be lower than what you have with your one-time close loan. At the end of the construction period, you can simply use your VA loan to refinance the construction note and not take the construction lender's higher permanent rate.

Refinancing

Another time to scrutinize using your VA entitlement is during a refinance.

If you bought your home a few years ago and rates have moved down, or you want to do a cash-out refinance, or you want to change the term of your loan, a VA loan might not be your best choice, primarily because of your funding fee.

We touched on this topic briefly in Chapter 7, but remember that funding fees are attached to all VA loans and can get pretty expensive during a refinance. When you refinance a VA loan, that funding fee can be as high as 3.3 percent, based upon usage and type of service.

A funding fee will be charged on cash-out refinances, or if the new loan goes to pay off any previous second mortgage or home equity line of credit (HELOC). If the refinance is not a cash out and is just an Interest Rate Reduction Loan (IRRL), the funding fee drops to one-half percent.

Either way, you can't avoid the funding fee. If you have built up equity in your home and you want to refinance for any reason, consider the funding fee associated with your VA loan.

You may want to refinance into a conventional loan. Conventional mortgages are the most common mortgage type and have the same loan limits VA loans do. But they do not require a funding fee. They do, however, require a mortgage insurance premium if the first mortgage is above 80 percent of the appraised value.

Mortgage insurance is an insurance policy that pays the lender a portion of the loan balance should the borrower default. It works much the same way a VA loan works. If a borrower puts 5 percent down on a conventional mortgage and borrows 95 percent of the sales price, a mortgage insurance policy is required, and the payment is usually in the form of a monthly premium.

If a home sells for $400,000 and the borrower puts 5 percent down, that leaves a loan amount of $380,000. Although VA rates and conventional rates are typically the same, it's the mortgage insurance premium that shows up on a conventional loan.

In this example, the monthly mortgage insurance premium would be a whopping $278 per month. If the borrower put down 20 percent and kept the loan at $320,000, there would be no mortgage insurance premium. Although the VA has a funding fee, it's a far cry from the $278 mortgage insurance premium each month.

Let's compare:

Sales price = $400,000
Conventional with 5% down:
$380,000 loan amount, 30-year fixed, 6.00%
    Monthly payment $2,267
    Mortgage insurance $278
    Total $2,545

VA loan:
$408,000 loan amount (30-year fixed, 6.00% with 2.00% funding fee)
    Monthly payment $2,434

Conventional loans with mortgage insurance can't compare with VA loans, but when there's equity in the property in the case of a refinance, it shakes out differently.

Let's say your home is valued at $500,000, you have a $325,000 balance, and you want to borrow an additional $50,000 cash-out to make some home improvements. Now your funding fee would be 2.15 percent of the new loan amount, or:

$$\$375{,}000 \times 2.15 \text{ percent} = \$8{,}062.50$$

A conventional loan wouldn't require that $8,062.50 and would still give you the same rate. If you've gained some equity in your home, look at other options. When equity comes into play, the VA loan may not be your best bet.

If, however, you have trouble qualifying from a conventional standpoint and may have experienced recent credit problems and still want to cash-out refinance, the VA loan may be your only choice.

The very same way conventional loans with equity can be a better deal in a refinance, so too can they be competitive in a purchase when there is down payment involved.

Because of the funding fee, the VA loan is less desirable. However, if you find you can't qualify for a conventional loan due to credit and/or debt-ratio issues, then putting some money into a VA transaction enhances the likelihood of your approval.

Putting money into a VA transaction, say, 5 percent to 10 percent, can help you get approved on the very same loan if a conventional loan can't get you qualified. Try the VA loan using the lender's Automated Underwriting System (AUS) with down payment money to see if you can get approved. The VA is more forgiving in this manner.

It is certainly more forgiving when it comes to an IRRL. Only the mortgage needs to have been kept current in the previous twelve months, and no credit check is required. If your credit has been damaged and you have a VA loan, the VA may be your only and best source.

Cash-out refinancing? Consider other alternatives. No cash-out and simply reducing your rate? Hands down: IRRL.

Credit Issues and Subprime Lending

But what if your credit has been hurt so much that you currently can't get a VA approval? In this instance, you'd research "nonprime" lending.

Nonprime loans, sometimes called subprime loans, are so called because they're designed for people who have credit that is "less than prime." These loans are for people who have experienced recent credit issues or are currently experiencing bad credit times.

VA loans are not made to subprime borrowers; you still have to qualify from an income or credit perspective. If you find yourself in a situation where your credit has been damaged and you've found a house you want to buy, you can either wait for a couple of years to reestablish your credit or you can get a nonprime loan.

If you do get a nonprime loan, there are certain things you need to be aware of.

First and foremost, watch your back. And your front, for that matter. Nonprime loans, by their nature, aren't necessarily bad, but sometimes the people who issue them can be. You've probably heard the term *predatory lending,* and most often predators use nonprime loans to gouge their victims. Don't be one of them.

Nonprime lending makes up nearly one-quarter of all loans in the United States. That's a lot, and they have a place in the industry. Nonprime loans are designed for people who need a helping hand and whose credit has been damaged due to the loss of a job or a divorce or, worse, a death in the family.

Bad things can happen to good people, and sometimes the only way to help out these potential homeowners is to provide a mortgage to them when others won't. But taking advantage of someone during the process is evil, and it happens.

I used to do my fair share of nonprime loans, and it was gratifying to see people get back on their financial feet again after times of extended financial trouble. These people could have experienced a recent bankruptcy or had collection accounts or charge-offs; possibly even creditors could have taken them to court, sued for their credit card balances, and won a judgment. These are all bad things, but nonprime lenders pay less attention to them than conventional and VA lenders do.

When you get into a nonprime situation, the tendency may be to just go ahead and pay exorbitant rates and fees and move on down the road. But if you pay more than one point or one origination charge for a nonprime loan, you're getting taken advantage of.

Nonprime lenders may advertise that they specialize in lending to people with damaged credit, or you may call a loan officer there and he'll tell you he has a special program that only he has and can help you. But that's not the case at all. Nonprime mortgage loans have their very own secondary market, just like VA loans do with Ginnie Mae, or conventional loans have with Fannie Mae or Freddie Mac.

That means that all nonprime lenders offer the very same product. Or they usually do, anyway. So you can compare a nonprime loan from one lender to the next the same way you would when comparing potential VA suitors.

If there's one thing to keep in the forefront of your mind, it is that the nonprime mortgage is only supposed to be temporary and not a long-term solution. You really, really need to be thinking about "acquisition cost" when it comes to comparing nonprime mortgage loans.

First, do not pay any discount points or origination charges. Any lender, nonprime or VA, can calculate a "no point, no origination charge" loan by adjusting the rate upward, typically by one-quarter percent for each point the mortgage broker or nonprime lender makes on the loan.

Don't get taken by that kind of offer. They may say that because you're a very difficult loan, they have to charge more. That's a crock. Some loan officers will tell you that because they have to do so much and there are only a few places where that loan could be approved, you'll have to pay three points and some origination charges. That loan officer is also lying.

Where do you find nonprime lenders? They're everywhere. In fact, your very own bank may have a nonprime division. If you've been turned down by a VA lender, start with your very own bank or credit union. Call these people on the phone or shoot them an e-mail. Tell them your situation, your credit score, and so on, and if they have a nonprime division, you'll be transferred to that department and you'll deal with them from that point forward.

If you're working with mortgage bankers, they too have nonprime resources, as do mortgage brokers. Whichever source you choose, work with someone you have some degree of familiarity with, and don't go to companies that only work with people who have credit problems.

I've said this before and caught some flak about it, primarily from those very same companies that specialize in nonprime lending. They say they know more about nonprime than someone who only does VA loans. And they'd be right about that. It's just that in my experience, companies that only do nonprime loans make themselves out to be unique, and on that basis they claim to therefore command higher prices in the form of additional fees and points, and that is being less than honest.

Nonprime mortgage loans are a commodity, just like any other loan. That means you should shop them for the best deal like you would anything else.

Your strategy with nonprime loans should also include an exit strategy . . . the point when you refinance out of that loan into a new one with more competitive rates. And the most forgiving loan with normal rates is a VA loan with equity.

You can gain equity through normal appreciation in property values. If you're fortunate to live in an area with a 10 percent annual appreciation rate and you bought a home at $200,000, then the next year that home would be worth $220,000. Given a slight paydown on the current mortgage, you would be just under a 90 percent loan-to-value (LTV) ratio. That might be the time to give your 90 percent LTV VA refinance a shot—but only if you've begun to repair your credit by not having any more late payments, especially on your mortgage.

A one-year time frame might in fact be a little too short for credit to be repaired, but really only you would know that. Perhaps a two-year period would be better. Either way, it's important to know how nonprime loans are underwritten and approved.

First and foremost, nonprime loans are driven by your credit score whereas VA loans are not. VA loans do not require a minimum credit score, but nonprime loans certainly do.

Second, nonprime loans are also focused on equity. There are nonprime mortgage loans that have zero down but are only available for those with a certain minimum credit score. If your score falls below the minimum, you'll either have to wait or put an additional 5 percent down on the purchase. You can put more down or less down, and nonprime loans can change their rate and lending parameters accordingly.

The VA can be more lenient with more money down, but it is not as rigorous as nonprime lenders when it comes to lending parameters. VA lenders have a broader view when it comes to loan approval, taking all things into consideration, so one negative item by itself won't cause the VA lender to deny the loan. Nonprime lenders, by comparison, have serious issues with their loan requirements. If a loan requires a minimum credit score of 560, for instance, but someone comes in with a score of 559, the borrower would probably have to either borrow less money or put 5 percent more down.

Prepayment Penalties

Nonprime loans also can carry prepayment penalties, something you need to be fully aware of when taking a subprime loan.

A prepayment penalty is a predetermined amount of mortgage interest the lender will collect should you retire the loan early, either by refinancing or selling the property outright and paying off the mortgage along with it.

A prepayment penalty can be "hard" or "soft." A hard penalty means that no additional payments can be made whatsoever, otherwise you'll be charged a penalty. A soft penalty will allow you to make small prepayments on the note at any time, usually an amount that is no greater than 20 percent of the remaining principal balance. For example, on a $100,000 loan, you can pay up to 20 percent of the balance without incurring any penalty, or $20,000. On a hard penalty, if you paid extra, you could be liable for up to six months' interest penalty, or about $2,400, using an 8 percent nonprime rate.

Prepayment penalties can last for the entire life of the loan but are normally only for two- or three-year periods. After that, there is no prepayment penalty whatsoever. This prepayment period needs to be a significant part of your refinancing strategy when you move into a VA loan.

Additionally, most nonprime mortgages are what's called a "hybrid," which means a cross between a fixed rate and an ARM. That means your rate is fixed for either two or three years then turns into an ARM, amortized over thirty years. A 2/28 loan is fixed for two years then turns into an ARM for the next twenty-eight years, with higher than normal margins, making nonprime mortgage rates higher than those reserved for VA loans.

Hybrids can come in a variety of formats: fixed for two years, three years, five years, and so on. Your strategy should be to match up your hybrid term with your prepayment penalty term.

If your goal is to repair your credit within about twenty-four months, then take the 2/28 loan (which gives you a lower rate) and a two-year prepayment penalty. If you select a 3/27 loan, then choose the three-year prepayment penalty.

If your goal is to repair and reestablish your credit during that two- or three-year period, then refinance. If you're not sure you can do all of that in twenty-four months, then take the 3/27 loan.

Investment Properties

You can't use your VA loan to buy investment property. If you want to buy a rental house or even a vacation home somewhere, your VA entitlement won't allow for it. The VA loan is for your primary residence and nothing else.

If, however, you currently have a VA loan and have accrued some equity over the years, a good way to buy a rental house or other investment property would be to use the equity in your primary home as a down payment on the rental property.

Mortgages on investment properties will have slightly higher rates and ask for more down payment than those for primary residences. If there's a house you want to buy as a rental, you can use funds from your bank account or, if you want to leave those savings alone, get an equity loan. The cheapest rates on mortgage money come from primary residences.

Not Ready

Finally, another time not to use your VA entitlement is when you're simply not ready to buy. Once word gets out that you're thinking about buying a home, it seems every loan officer, real estate agent, or cousin-in-law wants to start showing you houses.

If you don't watch out, you'll be rushed into doing something you're not sure you want to do. It's okay to get butterflies or second-guess your decision, that's normal; but don't get pushed into anything you're not ready for.

Remember, you're the one in control. You're the veteran. Thank you for all you've done.

Appendix A: VA Regional Loan Centers

Regional Loan Center	Jurisdiction	Mailing and Website Addresses	Telephone Number
Atlanta	Georgia North Carolina South Carolina Tennessee	Department of Veterans Affairs Regional Loan Center 1700 Clairmont Rd. P.O. Box 100023 Decatur, GA 30031-7023 www.vba.va.gov/ro/atlanta/rlc/ index.htm	1-888-768-2132
Cleveland	Delaware Indiana Michigan New Jersey Ohio Pennsylvania	Department of Veterans Affairs Cleveland Regional Loan Center 1240 East Ninth Street Cleveland, OH 44199 www.vba.va.gov/ro/central/cleve/ index1.htm	1-800-729-5772
Denver	Alaska Colorado Idaho Montana Oregon Utah Washington Wyoming	Department of Veterans Affairs VA Regional Loan Center Box 25126 Denver, CO 80225 www.vba.va.gov/ro/denver/loan/ lgy.htm	1-888-349-7541
Honolulu	Hawaii	Department of Veterans Affairs Loan Guaranty Division (26) 459 Patterson Rd. Honolulu, HI 96819 *Although not an RLC, this office is a fully functioning Loan Guaranty operation for Hawaii.	1-808-433-0481
Houston	Arkansas Louisiana Oklahoma Texas	Department of Veterans Affairs VA Regional Loan Center 6900 Alameda Road Houston, TX 77030 http://www.vba.va.gov/houston rlc.htm	1-888-232-2571
Manchester	Connecticut Massachusetts Maine New Hampshire New York Rhode Island Vermont	Department of Veterans Affairs VA Regional Loan Center 275 Chestnut Street Manchester, NH 03101 www.vba.va.gov/ro/manchester/ lgymain/loans.html	1-800-827-6311 1-800-827-0336

Phoenix	Arizona California New Mexico Nevada	Department of Veterans Affairs VA Regional Loan Center 3333 N. Central Avenue Phoenix, AZ 85012–2436 www.vba.va.gov/phoenixlgy.htm	1-888-869-0194
Roanoke	District of Columbia Kentucky Maryland Virginia West Virginia	Department of Veterans Affairs Roanoke Regional Loan Center 210 Franklin Road SW Roanoke, VA 24011 http://www.vba.va.gov/ro/roanoke/ rlc	1-800-933-5499
St. Paul	Illinois Iowa Kansas Minnesota Missouri Nebraska North Dakota South Dakota Wisconsin	Department of Veterans Affairs VA Regional Loan Center 1 Federal Drive Fort Snelling, St. Paul, MN 55111 http://www.vba.va.gov/ro/central/ stpau/pages/homeloans.html	1-800-827-0611
St. Petersburg	Alabama Florida Mississippi Puerto Rico U.S. Virgin Islands	Department of Veterans Affairs VA Regional Loan Center P.O. Box 1437 St. Petersburg, FL 33731-1437 http://www.vba.va.gov/ro/south/ spete/rlc/index.htm	1-888-611-5916 (out of state) 1-800-827-1000 (in FL)

Appendix B: VA Contact Information

State	VA Contact Information
Alabama	Alabama Dept. of Veterans Affairs Suite 530 770 Washington Avenue Montgomery, AL 36130 (334) 242–5077
Alaska	Alaska Housing Finance Corporation P.O. Box 101020 Anchorage, AK 99510–1020 (800) 478–2432
Arizona	Arizona Dept. of Veterans Services 4141 North 3rd Street Phoenix, AZ 85012 (602) 255–3373
Arkansas	Arkansas Dept. of Veterans Affairs 2200 Fort Roots Drive Bldg. 65, Rm. 119 North Little Rock, AR 72114 (501) 370–3820
California	California Dept. of Veterans Affairs Veterans Home Division 1227 "O" Street Sacramento, CA 95814 (800) 952–5626
Colorado	Colorado Division of Veterans Affairs Office 789 Sherman Street Suite 260 Denver, CO 80203 (303) 894–7424

Connecticut   Connecticut Dept. of Veterans Affairs
                   287 West Street
                   Rocky Hill, CT 06067
                   (860) 529–2571
                   (800) 550–0000

Delaware   Delaware Commission of Veterans Affairs
                   Robbins Bldg.
                   802 Silver Lake Blvd., Suite 100
                   Dover, DE 19904
                   (302) 739–2792

Florida   FDVA Executive Office
                   4040 Esplanade Way, Suite 152
                   Tallahassee, FL 32399–0950
                   (850) 487–1533

Georgia   Georgia Veterans Affairs
                   Floyd Veterans Memorial Building
                   205 Butler Street
                   Suite E-970
                   Atlanta, GA 30334–4800
                   (404) 656–2300

Hawaii   Hawaii Office of Veterans Services
                   459 Patterson Road, E-Wing, room 1-A103
                   Honolulu, HI 96819
                   (808) 433–0420

Idaho   Idaho State Veterans Services
                   320 Collins Road
                   Boise, ID 83702
                   (208) 334–3513

Illinois   Illinois Dept. of Veterans Affairs
                   JRTC
                   100 West Randolph, Suite 5–570
                   Chicago, IL 60601–3219
                   (312) 814–2460

Indiana   Indiana Dept. of Veterans Affairs
                   302 W. Washington Street, Room E-120

	Indianapolis, IN 46204–2738 (317) 232–3910
Iowa	Camp Dodge, Bldg A6A 7105 NW 70th Avenue Johnston, IA 50131–1824 (515) 242–5331
Kansas	Kansas Commission on Veterans Affairs Jayhawk Tower 700 Southwest Jackson, Suite 701 Topeka, KS 66603–3743 (785) 296–3976
Kentucky	Kentucky Dept. of Veterans Affairs 1111 Louisville Road Frankfort, KY 40601 (502) 564–9203
Louisiana	Louisiana Dept. of Veterans Affairs 1885 Wooddale Boulevard P.O. Box 94095 Baton Rouge, LA 70804–9095 (225) 922–0500
Maine	Maine Bureau of Veterans Services 117 State House Station Augusta, ME 04333 (207) 626–4464
Maryland	Maryland Dept. of Veterans Affairs The Jeffrey Bldg., 4th Floor 16 Francis Street Annapolis, MD 21401 (410) 260–3838
Massachusetts	Commonwealth of Massachusetts Dept. of Veterans Affairs 600 Washington Street, Suite 1100 Boston, MA 02111 (617) 210–5480

Michigan   Michigan Dept. of Military and Veterans Affairs
                    7109 W. Saginaw
                    Lansing, MI 48913
                    (517) 335–6523

Minnesota   Minnesota Dept. of Veterans Affairs
                    20 West 12th Street
                    St. Paul, MN 55155
                    (651) 296–2562

Mississippi   Mississippi Veterans' Home Purchase Board
                    3466 Highway 80 East
                    Pearl, MS 39208
                    (601) 576–4800

Missouri   Missouri Veterans Commission
                    205 Jefferson Street
                    12th Floor, Jefferson Building
                    P.O. Drawer 147
                    Jefferson City, MO 65102
                    (573) 751–3779

Montana   Montana Veterans Affairs
                    Helena Armed Forces Reserve Center
                    1900 Williams Street
                    P.O. Box 5715
                    Helena, MT 59604
                    (406) 324–3740

Nebraska   Nebraska Dept. of Veterans Affairs
                    P.O. Box 95083
                    301 Centennial Mall South, 6th Floor
                    Lincoln, NE 68509–5083
                    (402) 471–2458

Nevada   Nevada Office of Veterans' Services
                    5460 Reno Corporate Drive
                    Reno, NV 89511
                    (775) 688–1653

New Hampshire 275 Chestnut Street, Room 517
               Manchester, NH 03101–2411
               (603) 624–9230
               (800) 622–9230

New Jersey   New Jersey Veterans
               Eggerts Crossing Road
               P.O. Box 340
               Trenton, NJ 08625–0340
               (800) 624–0508

New Mexico   New Mexico Dept. of Veterans Services
               Bataan Memorial Building
               407 Galistco, Room 142
               Santa Fe, NM 87501
               (505) 827–6300

New York   NYS Division of Veterans Affairs
               #5 Empire State Plaza
               Suite 2836
               Albany, NY 12223–1551
               (888) 838-7697

North Carolina Division of Veterans Affairs
               325 North Salisbury Street
               Albemarle Bldg., Suite 1065
               Raleigh, NC 27603
               (919) 733–3851

North Dakota   North Dakota Veterans Affairs
               1411 32nd Street South
               P.O. Box 9003
               Fargo, ND 58106–9003
               (866) 634–8387

Ohio   Governor's Office of Veterans Affairs
               77 South High Street
               Columbus, OH 43215
               (614) 644–0898

Oklahoma   Oklahoma Dept. of Veterans Affairs
                  2311 North Central
                  Oklahoma City, OK 73105
                  (405) 521–3684

Oregon   Oregon Dept. of Veterans Affairs
                  700 Summer Street NE
                  Salem, OR 97301–1285
                  (503) 373–2000

Pennsylvania   Pennsylvania Dept. of Military and Veterans Affairs
                  Bureau for Veterans Affairs
                  Fort Indiantown Gap, Bldg. S-0–47
                  Annville, PA 17003
                  (800) 547–2838

Rhode Island   The Veterans Affairs Office
                  480 Metacom Avenue
                  Bristol, RI 02809
                  (401) 462–0324

South Carolina   Governor's Office
                  South Carolina Office of Veterans Affairs
                  1205 Pendleton Street, Suite 369
                  Columbia, SC 29201
                  (803) 734–0200

South Dakota   Soldiers and Sailors Memorial Building
                  425 East Capitol Avenue
                  Pierre, SD 57501–5070
                  (605) 773–3269

Tennessee   Tennessee Dept. of Veterans Affairs
                  215 Eighth Avenue North
                  Nashville, TN 37243
                  (615) 741–6663

Texas   Veterans Affairs Headquarters
                  P.O. Box 12277
                  Stephen F. Austin Building, Suite 620

Austin, TX 78711–2277
(512) 463–5538

Utah   Utah Division of Veterans' Affairs
                550 Foothill Boulevard, #202
                Salt Lake City, UT 84108
                (801) 326–2372

Vermont   State of Vermont Office of Veterans Affairs
                118 State Street, Drawer 20
                Montpelier, VT 05620
                (802) 828–3379

Virginia   Dept. of Veterans Services
                Office of the Commissioner
                900 E. Main Street
                Richmond, VA 23219
                (804) 786–0286

Washington   Washington State Department of Veterans Affairs
                1102 Quince Street SE
                3rd Floor
                P.O. Box 41150
                Olympia, WA 98504
                (800) 562–0132

West Virginia   West Virginia Division of Veterans Affairs
                1321 Plaza East, Suite 101
                Charleston, WV 25301
                (304) 558–3661

Wisconsin   Wisconsin Dept. of Veterans Affairs
                30 W. Mifflin Street
                Madison, WI 53703
                (608) 266–1311

Wyoming   Wyoming Veterans Commission
                5905 Cy Avenue, Room 101
                Casper, WY 82604
                (307) 265–7372

Appendix C: Request for Certificate of Eligibility

OMB Approved No. 2900-0086
Respondent Burden: 15 minutes

VA Department of Veterans Affairs **REQUEST FOR A CERTIFICATE OF ELIGIBILITY**	TO	Department of Veterans Affairs Attn: Loan Guaranty Division

NOTE: Please read information on reverse before completing this form. If additional space is required, attach a separate sheet.

1. FIRST-MIDDLE-LAST NAME OF VETERAN	2. DATE OF BIRTH	3. VETERAN'S DAYTIME TELEPHONE NO. ( )

4. ADDRESS OF VETERAN (No., street or rural route, city or P.O., State and ZIP Code)	5. MAIL CERTIFICATE OF ELIGIBILITY TO: (Complete ONLY if the Certificate is to be mailed to an address different from the one listed in Item 4)

6. MILITARY SERVICE DATA (ATTACH PROOF OF SERVICE - SEE PARAGRAPH "D" ON REVERSE)

A. ITEM	B. PERIODS OF ACTIVE SERVICE		C. NAME (Show your name exactly as it appears on your separation papers or Statement of Service	D. SOCIAL SECURITY NUMBER	E. SERVICE NUMBER (If different from Social Security No.)	F. BRANCH OF SERVICE
	DATE FROM	DATE TO				
1.						
2.						
3.						
4.						

7A. WERE YOU DISCHARGED, RETIRED OR SEPARATED FROM SERVICE BECAUSE OF DISABILITY OR DO YOU NOW HAVE ANY SERVICE-CONNECTED DISABILITIES?

☐ YES ☐ NO (If "Yes," complete Item 7B)

7B. VA CLAIM FILE NUMBER

C-

8. PREVIOUS VA LOANS (Must answer N/A if no previous VA home loan. DO NOT LEAVE BLANK)

A. ITEM	B. TYPE (Home, Refinance, Manufactured Home, or Direct)	C. ADDRESS OF PROPERTY	D. DATE OF LOAN	E. DO YOU STILL OWN THE PROPERTY? (YES/NO)	F. DATE PROPERTY WAS SOLD (Submit a copy of HUD-1, Settlement Statement, if available)	G. VA LOAN NUMBER (If known)
1.						
2.						
3.						
4.						
5.						
6.						

I CERTIFY THAT the statements herein are true to the best of my knowledge and belief.

9. SIGNATURE OF VETERAN (Do NOT print)	10. DATE SIGNED

FEDERAL STATUTES PROVIDE SEVERE PENALTIES FOR FRAUD, INTENTIONAL MISREPRESENTATION, CRIMINAL CONNIVANCE OR CONSPIRACY PURPOSED TO INFLUENCE THE ISSUANCE OF ANY GUARANTY OR INSURANCE BY THE SECRETARY OF VETERANS AFFAIRS.

FOR VA USE ONLY

11A. DATE CERTIFICATE ISSUED	11B. SIGNATURE OF VA AGENT

VA FORM FEB 2000 **26-1880**   SUPERSEDES VA FORM 26-1880, MAR 1999, WHICH WILL NOT BE USED.

Appendix D: Request Pertaining to Military Records

Standard Form 180 (Rev. 10-05) (Page 1)
Prescribed by NARA (36 CFR 1228.168(b))

Authorized for local reproduction
Previous edition unusable

OMB No. 3095-0029 Expires 9/30/2008

REQUEST PERTAINING TO MILITARY RECORDS

To ensure the best possible service, please thoroughly review the accompanying instructions before filling out this form. Please print clearly or type. If you need more space, use plain paper.

SECTION I - INFORMATION NEEDED TO LOCATE RECORDS (Furnish as much as possible.)

1. NAME USED DURING SERVICE (last, first, and middle)	2. SOCIAL SECURITY NO.	3. DATE OF BIRTH	4. PLACE OF BIRTH

5. SERVICE , PAST AND PRESENT   (For an effective records search, it is important that all service be shown below.)

| BRANCH OF SERVICE | DATES OF SERVICE | | CHECK ONE | | SERVICE NUMBER DURING THIS PERIOD |
	DATE ENTERED	DATE RELEASED	OFFICER	ENLISTED	(If unknown, write "unknown")
a. ACTIVE SERVICE					
b. RESERVE SERVICE					
c. NATIONAL GUARD					

6. IS THIS PERSON DECEASED? If "YES" enter the date of death.
☐ NO   ☐ YES _____

7. IS (WAS) THIS PERSON RETIRED FROM MILITARY SERVICE?
☐ NO   ☐ YES

SECTION II – INFORMATION AND/OR DOCUMENTS REQUESTED

1. REPORT OF SEPARATION (DD Form 214 or equivalent). This contains information normally needed to verify military service. A copy may be sent to the veteran, the deceased veteran's next of kin, or other persons or organizations if authorized in Section III, below. NOTE. If more than one period of service was performed, even in the same branch, there may be more than one Report of Separation. Be sure to show EACH year that a Report of Separation was issued, for which you need a copy.

☐ An **UNDELETED** Report of Separation is requested for the year(s) _____

This normally will be a copy of the full separation document including such sensitive items as the character of separation, authority for separation, reason for separation, reenlistment eligibility code, separation (SPD/SPN) code, and dates of time lost. An undeleted version is ordinarily required to determine eligibility for benefits.

☐ A **DELETED** Report of Separation is requested for the year(s) _____

The following information will be deleted from the copy sent: authority for separation, reason for separation, reenlistment eligibility code, separation(SPD/SPN) code, and for separations after June 30, 1979, character of separation and dates of time lost.

2. OTHER INFORMATION AND/OR DOCUMENTS REQUESTED _____

3. PURPOSE (Optional – An explanation of the purpose of the request is strictly voluntary. Such information may help the agency answering this request to provide the best possible response and will in no way be used to make a decision to deny the request.) _____

SECTION III - RETURN ADDRESS AND SIGNATURE

1. REQUESTER IS:

☐ Military service member or veteran identified in Section I, above

☐ Next of kin of deceased veteran _____
(relation)

☐ Legal guardian (must submit copy of court appointment)

☐ Other (specify) _____

2. SEND INFORMATION/DOCUMENTS TO:
(Please print or type. See item 3 on accompanying instructions.)

3. AUTHORIZATION SIGNATURE REQUIRED (See item 2 on accompanying instructions.) I declare (or certify, verify, or state) under penalty of perjury under the laws of the United States of America that the information in this Section III is true and correct.

Name _____

Signature   (Please do not print.) _____

Street _____ Apt. ____

(___) _____
Date of this request   Daytime phone

City _____ State ____ Zip Code ____

Email address _____

** This form is available at http://www.archives.gov/research/order/standard-form-180.pdf on the National Archives and Records Administration (NARA) web site. **

Standard Form 180 (Rev. 10-05) (Page 2)
Prescribed by NARA (36 CFR 1228.168(b))

Authorized for local reproduction
Previous edition unusable

OMB No. 3095-0029 Expires 9/30/2008

LOCATION OF MILITARY RECORDS

The various categories of military service records are described in the chart below. For each category there is a code number which indicates the address at the bottom of the page to which this request should be sent. Please refer to the Instruction and Information Sheet accompanying this form as needed.

BRANCH	CURRENT STATUS OF SERVICE MEMBER	ADDRESS CODE Personnel Record	Health Record
AIR FORCE	Discharged, deceased, or retired before 5/1/1994	14	14
	Discharged, deceased, or retired 5/1/1994 – 9/30/2004	14	11
	Discharged, deceased, or retired on or after 10/1/2004	1	11
	Active (including National Guard on active duty in the Air Force), TDRL, or general officers retired with pay	1	
	Reserve, retired reserve in nonpay status, current National Guard officers not on active duty in the Air Force, or National Guard released from active duty in the Air Force	2	
	Current National Guard enlisted not on active duty in the Air Force	13	
COAST GUARD	Discharge , deceased, or retired before 1/1/1898	6	
	Discharged, deceased, or retired 1/1/1898 – 3/31/1998	14	14
	Discharged, deceased, or retired on or after 4/1/1998	14	11
	Active, reserve, or TDRL	3	
MARINE CORPS	Discharged, deceased, or retired before 1/1/1905	6	
	Discharged, deceased, or retired 1/1/1905 – 4/30/1994	14	14
	Discharged, deceased, or retired 5/1/1994 – 12/31/1998	14	11
	Discharged, deceased, or retired on or after 1/1/1999	4	11
	Individual Ready Reserve or Fleet Marine Corps Reserve	5	
	Active, Selected Marine Corps Reserve, TDRL	4	
ARMY	Discharged, deceased, or retired before 11/1/1912 (enlisted) or before 7/1/1917 (officer)	6	
	Discharged, deceased, or retired 11/1/1912 – 10/15/1992 (enlisted) or 7/1/1917 – 10/15/1992 (officer)	14	14
	Discharged, deceased, or retired 10/16/1992 – 9/30/2002	14	11
	Discharged, deceased, or retired on or after 10/1/2002	7	11
	Reserve; or active duty records of current National Guard members who performed service in the U.S. Army before 7/1/1972	7	
	Active enlisted (including National Guard on active duty in the U.S. Army) or TDRL enlisted	9	
	Active officers (including National Guard on active duty in the U.S. Army) or TDRL officers	8	
	Current National Guard enlisted not on active duty in Army (including records of Army active duty performed after 6/30/1972)	13	
	Current National Guard officers not on active duty in Army (including records of Army active duty performed after 6/30/1972)	12	
NAVY	Discharged, deceased, or retired before 1/1/1886 (enlisted) or before 1/1/1903 (officer)	6	
	Discharged, deceased, or retired 1/1/1886 – 1/30/1994 (enlisted) or 1/1/1903 – 1/30/1994 (officer)	14	14
	Discharged, deceased, or retired 1/31/1994 – 12/31/1994	14	11
	Discharged, deceased, or retired on or after 1/1/1995	10	11
	Active, reserve, or TDRL	10	
PHS	Public Health Service - Commissioned Corps officers only	15	

ADDRESS LIST OF CUSTODIANS (BY CODE NUMBERS SHOWN ABOVE) – Where to write/send this form

1	Air Force Personnel Center HQ AFPC/DPSRP 550 C Street West, Suite 19 Randolph AFB, TX 78150-4721	6	National Archives & Records Administration Old Military and Civil Records (NWCTB-Military) Textual Services Division 700 Pennsylvania Ave., N.W. Washington, DC 20408-0001	11	Department of Veterans Affairs Records Management Center P.O. Box 5020 St. Louis, MO 63115-5020
2	Air Reserve Personnel Center /DSMR HQ ARPC/DPSSA/B 6760 E. Irvington Place, Suite 4600 Denver, CO 80280-4600	7	U.S. Army Human Resources Command ATTN: AHRC-PAV-V 1 Reserve Way St. Louis, MO 63132-5200	12	Army National Guard Readiness Center NGB-ARP 111 S. George Mason Dr. Arlington, VA 22204-1382
3	Commander, CGPC-adm-3 USCG Personnel Command 4200 Wilson Blvd., Suite 1100 Arlington, VA 22203-1804	8	U.S. Army Human Resources Command ATTN: AHRC-MSR 200 Stovall Street Alexandria, VA 22332-0444	13	The Adjutant General (of the appropriate state, DC, or Puerto Rico)
4	Headquarters U.S. Marine Corps Personnel Management Support Branch (MMSB-10) 2008 Elliot Road Quantico, VA 22134-5030	9	Commander USAEREC ATTN: PCRE-F 8899 E. 56th St. Indianapolis, IN 46249-5301	14	National Personnel Records Center (Military Personnel Records) 9700 Page Ave. St. Louis, MO 63132-5100
5	Marine Corps Reserve Support Command (Code MMI) 15303 Andrews Road Kansas City, MO 64147-1207	10	Navy Personnel Command (PERS-313C1) 5720 Integrity Drive Millington, TN 38055-3130	15	Division of Commissioned Corps Officer Support ATTN: Records Officer 1101 Wooton Parkway, Plaza Level, Suite 100 Rockville, MD 20852

Appendix E: Uniform Residential Loan Application

Uniform Residential Loan Application

This application is designed to be completed by the applicant(s) with the Lender's assistance. Applicants should complete this form as "Borrower" or "Co-Borrower", as applicable. Co-Borrower information must also be provided (and the appropriate box checked) when ☐ the income or assets of a person other than the "Borrower" (including the Borrower's spouse) will be used as a basis for loan qualification or ☐ the income or assets of the Borrower's spouse or other person who has community property rights pursuant to state law will not be used as a basis for loan qualification, but his or her liabilities must be considered because the spouse or other person has community property rights pursuant to applicable law and Borrower resides in a community property state, the security property is located in a community property state, or the Borrower is relying on other property located in a community property state as a basis for repayment of the loan.

If this is an application for joint credit, Borrower and Co-Borrower each agree that we intend to apply for joint credit (sign below):

Borrower _____ Co-Borrower _____

I. TYPE OF MORTGAGE AND TERMS OF LOAN

Mortgage Applied for:	☑ VA ☐ FHA	☐ Conventional ☐ USDA/Rural Housing Service	☐ Other (explain):	Agency Case Number	Lender Case Number

Amount $	Interest Rate %	No. of Months	Amortization Type:	☑ Fixed Rate ☐ GPM	☐ Other (explain): ☐ ARM (type):

II. PROPERTY INFORMATION AND PURPOSE OF LOAN

Subject Property Address (street, city, state, & ZIP)	No. of Units

Legal Description of Subject Property (attach description if necessary)	Year Built

Purpose of Loan	☑ Purchase ☐ Construction ☐ Refinance ☐ Construction-Permanent	☐ Other (explain):	Property will be: ☑ Primary Residence ☐ Secondary Residence ☐ Investment

Complete this line if construction or construction-permanent loan.

Year Lot Acquired	Original Cost $	Amount Existing Liens $	(a) Present Value of Lot $	(b) Cost of Improvements $	Total (a+b) $

Complete this line if this is a refinance loan.

Year Acquired	Original Cost $	Amount Existing Liens $	Purpose of Refinance	Describe Improvements ☐ made ☐ to be made Cost $

Title will be held in what Name(s)	Manner in which Title will be held	Estate will be held in: ☑ Fee Simple ☐ Leasehold (show expiration date)

Source of Down Payment, Settlement Charges and/or Subordinate Financing (explain)

III. BORROWER INFORMATION

Borrower	Co-Borrower
Borrower's Name (include Jr. or Sr. if applicable)	Co-Borrower's Name (include Jr. or Sr. if applicable)

Social Security Number	Home Phone (incl. area code)	DOB (mm/dd/yyyy)	Yrs. School	Social Security Number	Home Phone (incl. area code)	DOB (mm/dd/yyyy)	Yrs. School

☐ Married ☐ Separated ☐ Unmarried (include single, divorced, widowed)	Dependents (not listed by Co-Borrower) no. ages	☐ Married ☐ Separated ☐ Unmarried (include single, divorced, widowed)	Dependents (not listed by Borrower) no. ages

Present Address (street, city, state, ZIP) ☐ Own ☐ Rent ____ No. Yrs.	Present Address (street, city, state, ZIP) ☐ Own ☐ Rent ____ No. Yrs.

Mailing Address, if different from Present Address	Mailing Address, if different from Present Address

If residing at present address for less than two years, complete the following:

Former Address (street, city, state, ZIP) ☐ Own ☐ Rent ____ No. Yrs.	Former Address (street, city, state, ZIP) ☐ Own ☐ Rent ____ No. Yrs.
Former Address (street, city, state, ZIP) ☐ Own ☐ Rent ____ No. Yrs.	Former Address (street, city, state, ZIP) ☐ Own ☐ Rent ____ No. Yrs.

Fannie Mae Form 1003 07/05
CALYX Form Loanapp1.frm 09/05

Page 1 of 5

Borrower _____
Co-Borrower _____

Freddie Mac Form 65 07/05

181

	Borrower	IV. EMPLOYMENT INFORMATION		Co-Borrower	
Name & Address of Employer	☐ Self Employed	Yrs. on this job	Name & Address of Employer	☐ Self Employed	Yrs. on this job
		Yrs. employed in this line of work/profession			Yrs. employed in this line of work/profession
Position/Title/Type of Business		Business Phone (incl. area code)	Position/Title/Type of Business		Business Phone (incl. area code)

If employed in current position for less than two years or if currently employed in more than one position, complete the following:

Name & Address of Employer	☐ Self Employed	Dates (from-to)	Name & Address of Employer	☐ Self Employed	Dates (from-to)
		Monthly Income $			Monthly Income $
Position/Title/Type of Business		Business Phone (incl. area code)	Position/Title/Type of Business		Business Phone (incl. area code)
Name & Address of Employer	☐ Self Employed	Dates (from-to)	Name & Address of Employer	☐ Self Employed	Dates (from-to)
		Monthly Income $			Monthly Income $
Position/Title/Type of Business		Business Phone (incl. area code)	Position/Title/Type of Business		Business Phone (incl. area code)
Name & Address of Employer	☐ Self Employed	Dates (from-to)	Name & Address of Employer	☐ Self Employed	Dates (from-to)
		Monthly Income $			Monthly Income $
Position/Title/Type of Business		Business Phone (incl. area code)	Position/Title/Type of Business		Business Phone (incl. area code)
Name & Address of Employer	☐ Self Employed	Dates (from-to)	Name & Address of Employer	☐ Self Employed	Dates (from-to)
		Monthly Income $			Monthly Income $
Position/Title/Type of Business		Business Phone (incl. area code)	Position/Title/Type of Business		Business Phone (incl. area code)

V. MONTHLY INCOME AND COMBINED HOUSING EXPENSE INFORMATION

Gross Monthly Income	Borrower	Co-Borrower	Total	Combined Monthly Housing Expense	Present	Proposed
Base Empl. Income*	$	$	$	Rent	$	
Overtime				First Mortgage (P&I)		$
Bonuses				Other Financing (P&I)		
Commissions				Hazard Insurance		
Dividends/Interest				Real Estate Taxes		
Net Rental Income				Mortgage Insurance		
Other (before completing, see the notice in "describe other income," below)				Homeowner Assn. Dues		
				Other:		
Total	$	$	$	Total	$	$

* Self Employed Borrower(s) may be required to provide additional documentation such as tax returns and financial statements.

Describe Other Income   *Notice:* Alimony, child support, or separate maintenance income need not be revealed if the Borrower (B) or Co-Borrower (C) does not choose to have it considered for repaying this loan.

B/C		Monthly Amount
		$

VI. ASSETS AND LIABILITIES

This Statement and any applicable supporting schedules may be completed jointly by both married and unmarried Co-borrowers if their assets and liabilities are sufficiently joined so that the Statement can be meaningfully and fairly presented on a combined basis; otherwise, separate Statements and Schedules are required. If the Co-Borrower section was completed about a non-applicant spouse or other person, this Statement and supporting schedules must be completed by that spouse or other person also.

Completed ☑ Jointly ☐ Not Jointly

ASSETS Description	Cash or Market Value	Liabilities and Pledged Assets. List the creditor's name, address and account number for all outstanding debts, including automobile loans, revolving charge accounts, real estate loans, alimony, child support, stock pledges, etc. Use continuation sheet, if necessary. Indicate by (*) those liabilities which will be satisfied upon sale of real estate owned or upon refinancing of the subject property.		
Cash deposit toward purchase held by:	$	**LIABILITIES**	Monthly Payment & Months Left to Pay	Unpaid Balance
List checking and savings accounts below		Name and address of Company	$ Payment/Months	$
Name and address of Bank, S&L, or Credit Union				
		Acct. no.		
Acct. no.	$	Name and address of Company	$ Payment/Months	$
Name and address of Bank, S&L, or Credit Union				
		Acct. no.		
Acct. no.	$	Name and address of Company	$ Payment/Months	$
Name and address of Bank, S&L, or Credit Union				
		Acct. no.		
Acct. no.	$	Name and address of Company	$ Payment/Months	$
Stocks & Bonds (Company name/number description)	$			
		Acct. no.		
		Name and address of Company	$ Payment/Months	$
Life insurance net cash value	$			
Face amount $				
Subtotal Liquid Assets	$	Acct. no.		
Real estate owned (enter market value from schedule of real estate owned)	$	Name and address of Company	$ Payment/Months	$
Vested interest in retirement fund	$			
Net worth of business(es) owned (attach financial statement)	$	Acct. no.		
Automobiles owned (make and year)	$	Alimony/Child Support/Separate Maintenance Payments Owed to:	$	
Other Assets (itemize)	$	Job-Related Expense (child care, union dues, etc.)	$	
		Total Monthly Payments	$	
Total Assets a.	$	Net Worth ⇨ (a minus b)	$	**Total Liabilities b.** $

Schedule of Real Estate Owned (if additional properties are owned, use continuation sheet)

Property Address (enter S if sold, PS if pending sale or R if rental being held for income)	Type of Property	Present Market Value	Amount of Mortgages & Liens	Gross Rental Income	Mortgage Payments	Insurance, Maintenance, Taxes & Misc.	Net Rental Income
		$	$	$	$	$	$
Totals	$	$	$	$	$	$	$

List any additional names under which credit has previously been received and indicate appropriate creditor name(s) and account number(s):

Alternate Name	Creditor Name	Account Number

VII. DETAILS OF TRANSACTION		VIII. DECLARATIONS					
		If you answer "Yes" to any questions a through i, please use continuation sheet for explanation.		Borrower		Co-Borrower	
				Yes	No	Yes	No
a. Purchase price	$	a. Are there any outstanding judgments against you?		☐	☐	☐	☐
b. Alterations, improvements, repairs		b. Have you been declared bankrupt within the past 7 years?		☐	☐	☐	☐
c. Land (if acquired separately)		c. Have you had property foreclosed upon or given title or deed in lieu thereof in the last 7 years?		☐	☐	☐	☐
d. Refinance (incl. debts to be paid off)							
e. Estimated prepaid items		d. Are you a party to a lawsuit?		☐	☐	☐	☐
f. Estimated closing costs		e. Have you directly or indirectly been obligated on any loan which resulted in foreclosure, transfer of title in lieu of foreclosure, or judgment?		☐	☐	☐	☐
g. PMI, MIP, Funding Fee							
h. Discount (if Borrower will pay)		(This would include such loans as home mortgage loans, SBA loans, home improvement loans, educational loans, manufactured (mobile) home loans, any mortgage, financial obligation, bond, or loan guarantee. If "Yes," provide details, including date, name and address of Lender, FHA or VA case number, if any, and reasons for the action.)					
i. Total costs (add items a through h)							
j. Subordinate financing							
k. Borrower's closing costs paid by Seller		f. Are you presently delinquent or in default on any Federal debt or any other loan, mortgage, financial obligation, bond, or loan guarantee? If "Yes," give details as described in the preceding question.		☐	☐	☐	☐
l. Other Credits (explain)							
		g. Are you obligated to pay alimony, child support, or separate maintenance?		☐	☐	☐	☐
		h. Is any part of the down payment borrowed?		☐	☐	☐	☐
		i. Are you a co-maker or endorser on a note?		☐	☐	☐	☐
		j. Are you a U. S. citizen?		☐	☐	☐	☐
m. Loan amount (exclude PMI, MIP, Funding Fee financed)		k. Are you a permanent resident alien?		☐	☐	☐	☐
		l. Do you intend to occupy the property as your primary residence? If "Yes," complete question m below.		☐	☐	☐	☐
n. PMI, MIP, Funding Fee financed		m. Have you had an ownership interest in a property in the last three years?		☐	☐	☐	☐
o. Loan amount (add m & n)		(1) What type of property did you own-principal residence (PR), second home (SH), or investment property (IP)?		_____		_____	
p. Cash from/to Borrower (subtract j, k, l & o from i)		(2) How did you hold title to the home-solely by yourself (S), jointly with your spouse (SP), or jointly with another person (O)?		_____		_____	

IX. ACKNOWLEDGEMENT AND AGREEMENT

Each of the undersigned specifically represents to Lender and to Lender's actual or potential agents, brokers, processors, attorneys, insurers, servicers, successors and assigns and agrees and acknowledges that: (1) the information provided in this application is true and correct as of the date set forth opposite my signature and that any intentional or negligent misrepresentation of this information contained in this application may result in civil liability, including monetary damages, to any person who may suffer any loss due to reliance upon any misrepresentation that I have made on this application, and/or in criminal penalties including, but not limited to, fine or imprisonment or both under the provisions of Title 18, United States Code, Sec. 1001, et seq.; (2) the loan requested pursuant to this application (the "Loan") will be secured by a mortgage or deed of trust on the property described in this application; (3) the property will not be used for any illegal or prohibited purpose or use; (4) all statements made in this application are made for the purpose of obtaining a residential mortgage loan; (5) the property will be occupied as indicated in this application; (6) the Lender, its servicers, successors or assigns may retain the original and/or an electronic record of this application, whether or not the Loan is approved; (7) the Lender and its agents, brokers, insurers, servicers, successors and assigns may continuously rely on the information contained in the application, and I am obligated to amend and/or supplement the information provided in this application if any of the material facts that I have represented herein should change prior to closing of the Loan; (8) in the event that my payments on the Loan become delinquent, the Lender, its servicers, successors or assigns may, in addition to any other rights and remedies that it may have relating to such delinquency, report my name and account information to one or more consumer reporting agencies; (9) ownership of the Loan and/or administration of the Loan account may be transferred with such notice as may be required by law; (10) neither Lender nor its agents, brokers, insurers, servicers, successors or assigns has made any representation or warranty, express or implied, to me regarding the property or the condition or value of the property; and (11) my transmission of this application as an "electronic record" containing my "electronic signature," as those terms are defined in applicable federal and/or state laws (excluding audio and video recordings), or my facsimile transmission of this application containing a facsimile of my signature, shall be as effective, enforceable and valid as if a paper version of this application were delivered containing my original written signature.

Acknowledgement. Each of the undersigned hereby acknowledges that any owner of the Loan, its servicers, successors and assigns, may verify or reverify any information contained in this application or obtain any information or data relating to the Loan, for any legitimate purpose through any source, including a source named in this application or a consumer reporting agency.

Borrower's Signature X	Date	Co-Borrower's Signature X	Date

X. INFORMATION FOR GOVERNMENT MONITORING PURPOSES

The following information is requested by the Federal Government for certain types of loans related to a dwelling in order to monitor the lender's compliance with equal credit opportunity, fair housing and home mortgage disclosure laws. You are not required to furnish this information, but are encouraged to do so. The law provides that a Lender may not discriminate either on the basis of this information, or on whether you choose to furnish it. If you furnish the information, please provide both ethnicity and race. For race, you may check more than one designation. If you do not furnish ethnicity, race, or sex, under Federal regulations, this lender is required to note the information on the basis of visual observation and surname if you have made this application in person. If you do not wish to furnish the information, please check the box below. (Lender must review the above material to assure that the disclosures satisfy all requirements to which the lender is subject under applicable state law for the particular type of loan applied for.)

BORROWER	☐ I do not wish to furnish this information		CO-BORROWER	☐ I do not wish to furnish this information	
Ethnicity:	☐ Hispanic or Latino	☐ Not Hispanic or Latino	Ethnicity:	☐ Hispanic or Latino	☐ Not Hispanic or Latino
Race:	☐ American Indian or Alaska Native ☐ Asian ☐ Black or African American		Race:	☐ American Indian or Alaska Native ☐ Asian ☐ Black or African American	
	☐ Native Hawaiian or Other Pacific Islander ☐ White			☐ Native Hawaiian or Other Pacific Islander ☐ White	
Sex:	☐ Female	☐ Male	Sex:	☐ Female	☐ Male

To be Completed by Interviewer This application was taken by: ☐ Face-to-face interview ☐ Mail ☐ Telephone ☐ Internet	Interviewer's Name (print or type)		Name and Address of Interviewer's Employer
	Interviewer's Signature	Date	
	Interviewer's Phone Number (incl. area code)		

Continuation Sheet/Residential Loan Application

Use this continuation sheet if you need more space to complete the Residential Loan Application. Mark B for Borrower or C for Co-Borrower.	Borrower:	Agency Case Number:
	Co-Borrower:	Lender Case Number:

VI. ASSETS AND LIABILITIES

Schedule of Real Estate Owned

Property Address (enter S if sold, PS if pending sale or R if rental being held for income)	Type of Property	Present Market Value	Amount of Mortgages & Liens	Gross Rental Income	Mortgage Payments	Insurance, Maintenance, Taxes & Misc.	Net Rental Income

I/We fully understand that it is a Federal crime punishable by fine or imprisonment, or both, to knowingly make any false statements concerning any of the above facts as applicable under the provisions of Title 18, United States Code, Section 1001, et seq.

Borrower's Signature:	Date	Co-Borrower's Signature:	Date
X		X	

Appendix F: Payment Tables

The following tables will allow you to easily calculate your mortgage payments. First, find your interest rate in column one. Then move across to find the column that matches the term of your loan, then multiply that number by the number of thousand dollars financed. For example, let's say you have a 6.50 percent mortgage rate and a thirty-year term on a loan of $150,000. Your mortgage payment calculation would be:

$6.32 × 150 (thousands) = $948 (principal and interest payment)

Table 1. Payments per thousand dollars financed (forty-, thirty- and twenty-five-year terms).

Rate	40 Years	30 Years	25 Years
2.500	$3.30	$3.95	$4.49
2.625	$3.37	$4.02	$4.55
2.750	$3.44	$4.08	$4.61
2.875	$3.51	$4.15	$4.68
3.000	$3.58	$4.22	$4.74
3.125	$3.65	$4.28	$4.81
3.250	$3.73	$4.35	$4.87
3.375	$3.80	$4.42	$4.94
3.500	$3.87	$4.49	$5.01
3.625	$3.95	$4.56	$5.07
3.750	$4.03	$4.63	$5.14
3.875	$4.10	$4.70	$5.21
4.000	$4.18	$4.77	$5.28
4.125	$4.26	$4.85	$5.35
4.250	$4.34	$4.92	$5.42
4.125	$4.26	$4.85	$5.35
4.250	$4.34	$4.92	$5.42
4.375	$4.42	$4.99	$5.49
4.500	$4.50	$5.07	$5.56
4.625	$4.58	$5.14	$5.63
4.750	$4.66	$5.22	$5.70
4.875	$4.74	$5.29	$5.77
5.000	$4.82	$5.37	$5.85

Rate	40 Years	30 Years	25 Years
5.125	$4.91	$5.44	$5.92
5.250	$4.99	$5.52	$5.99
5.375	$5.07	$5.60	$6.07
5.500	$5.16	$5.68	$6.14
5.625	$5.24	$5.76	$6.22
5.750	$5.33	$5.84	$6.29
5.875	$5.42	$5.92	$6.37
6.000	$5.50	$6.00	$6.44
6.125	$5.59	$6.08	$6.52
6.250	$5.68	$6.16	$6.60
6.375	$5.77	$6.24	$6.67
6.500	$5.85	$6.32	$6.75
6.625	$5.94	$6.40	$6.83
6.750	$6.03	$6.49	$6.91
6.875	$6.12	$6.57	$6.99
7.000	$6.21	$6.65	$7.07
7.125	$6.31	$6.74	$7.15
7.250	$6.40	$6.82	$7.23
7.375	$6.49	$6.91	$7.31
7.500	$6.58	$6.99	$7.39
7.625	$6.67	$7.08	$7.47
7.750	$6.77	$7.16	$7.55
7.875	$6.86	$7.25	$7.64
8.000	$6.95	$7.34	$7.72
8.125	$7.05	$7.42	$7.80
8.250	$7.14	$7.51	$7.88
8.375	$7.24	$7.60	$7.97
8.500	$7.33	$7.69	$8.05
8.625	$7.43	$7.78	$8.14
8.750	$7.52	$7.87	$8.22
8.875	$7.62	$7.96	$8.31
9.000	$7.71	$8.05	$8.39
9.125	$7.81	$8.14	$8.48
9.250	$7.91	$8.23	$8.56
9.375	$8.00	$8.32	$8.65
9.500	$8.10	$8.41	$8.74
9.625	$8.20	$8.50	$8.82
9.750	$8.30	$8.59	$8.91

Table 1. (Continued)

Rate	40 Years	30 Years	25 Years
9.875	$8.39	$8.68	$9.00
10.000	$8.49	$8.78	$9.09
10.125	$8.59	$8.87	$9.18
10.250	$8.69	$8.96	$9.26
10.375	$8.79	$9.05	$9.35
10.500	$8.89	$9.15	$9.44
10.625	$8.98	$9.24	$9.53
10.750	$9.08	$9.33	$9.62
10.875	$9.18	$9.43	$9.71
11.000	$9.28	$9.52	$9.80
11.125	$9.38	$9.62	$9.89
11.250	$9.48	$9.71	$9.98
11.375	$9.58	$9.81	$10.07
11.500	$9.68	$9.90	$10.16
11.625	$9.78	$10.00	$10.26
11.750	$9.88	$10.09	$10.35
11.875	$9.98	$10.19	$10.44
12.000	$10.08	$10.29	$10.53
12.125	$10.19	$10.38	$10.62
12.250	$10.29	$10.48	$10.72
12.375	$10.39	$10.58	$10.81
12.500	$10.49	$10.67	$10.90
12.625	$10.59	$10.77	$11.00
12.750	$10.69	$10.87	$11.09
12.875	$10.79	$10.96	$11.18
13.000	$10.90	$11.06	$11.28
13.125	$11.00	$11.16	$11.37
13.250	$11.10	$11.26	$11.47
13.375	$11.20	$11.36	$11.56
13.500	$11.30	$11.45	$11.66
13.625	$11.40	$11.55	$11.75
13.750	$11.51	$11.65	$11.85
13.875	$11.61	$11.75	$11.94
14.000	$11.71	$11.85	$12.04
14.125	$11.81	$11.95	$12.13
14.250	$11.92	$12.05	$12.23
14.375	$12.02	$12.15	$12.33

Rate	40 Years	30 Years	25 Years
14.500	$12.12	$12.25	$12.42
14.625	$12.22	$12.35	$12.52
14.750	$12.33	$12.44	$12.61
14.875	$12.43	$12.54	$12.71
15.000	$12.53	$12.64	$12.81
15.125	$12.64	$12.74	$12.91
15.250	$12.74	$12.84	$13.00
15.375	$12.84	$12.94	$13.10
15.500	$12.94	$13.05	$13.20
15.625	$13.05	$13.15	$13.30
15.750	$13.15	$13.25	$13.39
15.875	$13.25	$13.35	$13.49
16.000	$13.36	$13.45	$13.59
16.125	$13.46	$13.55	$13.69
16.250	$13.56	$13.65	$13.79
16.375	$13.67	$13.75	$13.88
16.500	$13.77	$13.85	$13.98
16.625	$13.87	$13.95	$14.08
16.750	$13.98	$14.05	$14.18
16.875	$14.08	$14.16	$14.28
17.000	$14.18	$14.26	$14.38
17.125	$14.29	$14.36	$14.48
17.250	$14.39	$14.46	$14.58
17.375	$14.49	$14.56	$14.68
17.500	$14.60	$14.66	$14.78
17.625	$14.70	$14.77	$14.87
17.750	$14.80	$14.87	$14.97
17.875	$14.91	$14.97	$15.07
18.000	$15.01	$15.07	$15.17

Table 2. Payments per thousand dollars financed (twenty-, fifteen-, and ten-year terms).

Rate	20 Years	15 Years	10 Years
2.500	$5.30	$6.67	$9.43
2.625	$5.36	$6.73	$9.48
2.750	$5.42	$6.79	$9.54
2.875	$5.48	$6.85	$9.60
3.000	$5.55	$6.91	$9.66

Table 2. (Continued)

Rate	20 Years	15 Years	10 Years
3.125	$5.61	$6.97	$9.71
3.250	$5.67	$7.03	$9.77
3.375	$5.74	$7.09	$9.83
3.500	$5.80	$7.15	$9.89
3.625	$5.86	$7.21	$9.95
3.750	$5.93	$7.27	$10.01
3.875	$5.99	$7.33	$10.07
4.000	$6.06	$7.40	$10.12
4.125	$6.13	$7.46	$10.18
4.250	$6.19	$7.52	$10.24
4.125	$6.13	$7.46	$10.18
4.250	$6.19	$7.52	$10.24
4.375	$6.26	$7.59	$10.30
4.500	$6.33	$7.65	$10.36
4.625	$6.39	$7.71	$10.42
4.750	$6.46	$7.78	$10.48
4.875	$6.53	$7.84	$10.55
5.000	$6.60	$7.91	$10.61
5.125	$6.67	$7.97	$10.67
5.250	$6.74	$8.04	$10.73
5.375	$6.81	$8.10	$10.79
5.500	$6.88	$8.17	$10.85
5.625	$6.95	$8.24	$10.91
5.750	$7.02	$8.30	$10.98
5.875	$7.09	$8.37	$11.04
6.000	$7.16	$8.44	$11.10
6.125	$7.24	$8.51	$11.16
6.250	$7.31	$8.57	$11.23
6.375	$7.38	$8.64	$11.29
6.500	$7.46	$8.71	$11.35
6.625	$7.53	$8.78	$11.42
6.750	$7.60	$8.85	$11.48
6.875	$7.68	$8.92	$11.55
7.000	$7.75	$8.99	$11.61
7.125	$7.83	$9.06	$11.68
7.250	$7.90	$9.13	$11.74
7.375	$7.98	$9.20	$11.81

Rate	20 Years	15 Years	10 Years
7.500	$8.06	$9.27	$11.87
7.625	$8.13	$9.34	$11.94
7.750	$8.21	$9.41	$12.00
7.875	$8.29	$9.48	$12.07
8.000	$8.36	$9.56	$12.13
8.125	$8.44	$9.63	$12.20
8.250	$8.52	$9.70	$12.27
8.375	$8.60	$9.77	$12.33
8.500	$8.68	$9.85	$12.40
8.625	$8.76	$9.92	$12.47
8.750	$8.84	$9.99	$12.53
8.875	$8.92	$10.07	$12.60
9.000	$9.00	$10.14	$12.67
9.125	$9.08	$10.22	$12.74
9.250	$9.16	$10.29	$12.80
9.375	$9.24	$10.37	$12.87
9.500	$9.32	$10.44	$12.94
9.625	$9.40	$10.52	$13.01
9.750	$9.49	$10.59	$13.08
9.875	$9.57	$10.67	$13.15
10.000	$9.65	$10.75	$13.22
10.125	$9.73	$10.82	$13.28
10.250	$9.82	$10.90	$13.35
10.375	$9.90	$10.98	$13.42
10.500	$9.98	$11.05	$13.49
10.625	$10.07	$11.13	$13.56
10.750	$10.15	$11.21	$13.63
10.875	$10.24	$11.29	$13.70
11.000	$10.32	$11.37	$13.78
11.125	$10.41	$11.44	$13.85
11.250	$10.49	$11.52	$13.92
11.375	$10.58	$11.60	$13.99
11.500	$10.66	$11.68	$14.06
11.625	$10.75	$11.76	$14.13
11.750	$10.84	$11.84	$14.20
11.875	$10.92	$11.92	$14.27
12.000	$11.01	$12.00	$14.35
12.125	$11.10	$12.08	$14.42

Table 2. (Continued)

Rate	20 Years	15 Years	10 Years
12.250	$11.19	$12.16	$14.49
12.375	$11.27	$12.24	$14.56
12.500	$11.36	$12.33	$14.64
12.625	$11.45	$12.41	$14.71
12.750	$11.54	$12.49	$14.78
12.875	$11.63	$12.57	$14.86
13.000	$11.72	$12.65	$14.93
13.125	$11.80	$12.73	$15.00
13.250	$11.89	$12.82	$15.08
13.375	$11.98	$12.90	$15.15
13.500	$12.07	$12.98	$15.23
13.625	$12.16	$13.07	$15.30
13.750	$12.25	$13.15	$15.38
13.875	$12.34	$13.23	$15.45
14.000	$12.44	$13.32	$15.53
14.125	$12.53	$13.40	$15.60
14.250	$12.62	$13.49	$15.68
14.375	$12.71	$13.57	$15.75
14.500	$12.80	$13.66	$15.83
14.625	$12.89	$13.74	$15.90
14.750	$12.98	$13.83	$15.98
14.875	$13.08	$13.91	$16.06
15.000	$13.17	$14.00	$16.13
15.125	$13.26	$14.08	$16.21
15.250	$13.35	$14.17	$16.29
15.375	$13.45	$14.25	$16.36
15.500	$13.54	$14.34	$16.44
15.625	$13.63	$14.43	$16.52
15.750	$13.73	$14.51	$16.60
15.875	$13.82	$14.60	$16.67
16.000	$13.91	$14.69	$16.75
16.125	$14.01	$14.77	$16.83
16.250	$14.10	$14.86	$16.91
16.375	$14.19	$14.95	$16.99
16.500	$14.29	$15.04	$17.06
16.625	$14.38	$15.13	$17.14
16.750	$14.48	$15.21	$17.22

Rate	20 Years	15 Years	10 Years
16.875	$14.57	$15.30	$17.30
17.000	$14.67	$15.39	$17.38
17.125	$14.76	$15.48	$17.46
17.250	$14.86	$15.57	$17.54
17.375	$14.95	$15.66	$17.62
17.500	$15.05	$15.75	$17.70
17.625	$15.15	$15.84	$17.78
17.750	$15.24	$15.92	$17.86
17.875	$15.34	$16.01	$17.94
18.000	$15.43	$16.10	$18.02

Glossary

Abstract of Title   A written record of the historical ownership of the property, which helps to determine whether the property can, in fact, be transferred from one party to another without any previous claims. An abstract of title is used in certain parts of the country when determining if there are any previous claims on the subject property in question.

Acceleration   A loan accelerates when it is paid off early, usually at the request or demand of the lender. There is usually an associated acceleration clause within a loan document that states what must happen when a loan must be paid immediately, but most usually it applies to nonpayment, late payments, or transfer of the property without the lender's permission.

Adjustable-Rate Mortgage   A loan program where the interest rate may change throughout the life of the loan. It adjusts based on agreed-upon terms between the lender and the borrower but typically may only change once or twice a year.

Amortization   The length of time it takes before a loan is fully paid off, with repayment according to a predetermined agreement and at regular intervals. Sometimes called a *fully amortized* loan. Amortization terms can vary, but generally accepted terms run in five-year increments, from ten years to forty.

Appraisal   A report that helps to determine the market value of a property. It can be as simple or as detailed as necessary, as required by a lender: from simply driving by the property in a car to a full-blown inspection complete with full-color photographs of the real estate. Appraisals compare similar homes in the area in order to substantiate the value of the property in question.

APR   Annual Percentage Rate. The APR is the cost of money borrowed, expressed as an annual rate. The APR is a useful consumer tool to compare different lenders, but unfortunately, it is not used correctly. The APR can only work when comparing the same exact loan type from one lender to another. It doesn't work as well when comparing different types of mortgage programs with different down payments, terms, and so on.

Assumable Mortgage Homes sold with assumable mortgages let buyers take over the terms of the loan along with the house being sold. Assumable loans may be *fully or nonqualifying assumable*, meaning buyers take over the loan without being qualified or otherwise evaluated by the original lender. *Qualifying assumable* loans mean that although buyers may assume terms of the existing note, they must qualify all over again as if they were applying for a brand-new loan.

Automated Valuation Model An electronic method of evaluating a property's appraised value, done by scanning public records and other data for recent home sales in the subject property's neighborhood. This method is not yet widely accepted as a replacement for full-blown appraisals, but many within the industry expect AVMs to eventually replace traditional appraisals altogether.

Balloon Mortgage A type of mortgage where the remaining balance must be paid in full at the end of a preset term. A five-year balloon mortgage might be amortized over a thirty-year period but with the remaining balance due, in full, at the end of five years.

Bankers Lenders that use their own funds to lend money. Historically, these funds came from the savings accounts of other bank customers. But with the evolution of mortgage banking, that's the old way of doing business. Even though bankers use their own money, it may come from other sources, such as lines of credit or through selling loans to other institutions.

Basis Point One one-hundredth (1/100th) of a percent. Twenty-five basis points is one-fourth of a discount point; 100 basis points is one discount point.

Bridge Loan A short-term loan primarily used to pull equity out of one property for a down payment on another. This loan is paid off when the original property sells. Because they are short-term loans with sometimes just a few weeks before repayment, usually only retail banks will offer them. Usually the borrower doesn't make any monthly payments and only pays off the loan when the property sells.

Brokers   Mortgage companies that set up a home loan between a banker and a borrower. Brokers don't have money to lend directly, but they have experience in finding various loan programs that can suit the borrower. Similar to how independent insurance agents operate, brokers don't work for the borrower but instead provide mortgage loan choices from other mortgage lenders.

Bundling   The act of putting together several real estate or mortgage services in one package. Instead of paying for an appraisal here or an inspection there, you get some or all of the services packaged together. Usually bundling is done to offer discounts on all services, although when they're bundled it's hard to price all the services individually to see whether you're getting a good deal.

Buydown   Paying more money to get a lower interest rate. This is called a *permanent buydown,* and it is used in conjunction with discount points. The more points, the lower the rate. A *temporary buydown* is a fixed-rate mortgage that starts at a reduced rate for the first period and then gradually increases to its final note rate. A temporary buydown for two years is called a 2–1 buydown. For three years, it's called a 3-2-1 buydown.

Cash-Out   Taking equity out of a home in the form of cash during a refinance. Instead of just reducing your interest rate during a refinance and financing your closing costs, you finance even more, putting the money in your pocket.

Certificate of Eligibility   The VA form that tells you and your VA lender if you are eligible and how much VA entitlement you have available to use to buy or refinance using a VA loan. It is required on every VA mortgage.

Closing Costs   The various fees involved when buying a home or obtaining mortgage. The fees can come directly from the lender or may come from other transactions that are required to issue a good loan.

Collateral   Property owned by the borrower that's pledged to the lender, to be returned in case the loan goes bad. A lender makes a mortgage with the house as collateral.

Comparable Sales   Part of an appraisal report, it lists recent transfers of similar properties in the immediate area of the house being bought. Also called "comps."

Conforming Loan   A conventional conforming loan eligible for sale to Fannie Mae or Freddie Mac and is equal to or less than the maximum allowable loans limits established by the Federal National Mortgage Association and Federal Home Loan Mortgage Corporation, respectively. These limits are changed annually.

Conventional Loan   A mortgage using guidelines established by Fannie Mae or Freddie Mac and issued and guaranteed by lenders.

Credit Report   A report showing the payment histories of a consumer, along with the consumer's property addresses and certain public records.

DD-214   VA form number that shows your discharge information from the armed services.

Debt Consolidation   Paying off all or part of one's consumer debt with equity from a home. It can be done as part of a refinanced mortgage or a separate equity loan.

Debt Ratio   Gross monthly payments divided by gross monthly income, expressed as a percentage. There are typically two debt ratios to be considered: Housing ratio—sometimes called the *front ratio*—is the total monthly house payment plus any monthly tax, insurance, private mortgage insurance, or homeowners association dues, divided by gross monthly income. The total debt ratio—also called the *back ratio*—is the total housing payment plus other monthly consumer installment or revolving debt, also expressed as a percentage. Loan debt-ratio guidelines are usually denoted as 32/ 38, with 32 being the front ratio and the 38 being the back ratio. Ratio guidelines can vary from loan to loan and lender to lender.

Deed   A written document evidencing each transfer of ownership in a property.

Deed of Trust   A written document giving an interest in the home being bought to a third party, usually the lender, as security to the lender.

Delinquent   Being behind on a mortgage payment. Delinquencies are typically categorized as 30 + days delinquent, 60 + days delinquent, and 90 + days delinquent.

Discount Points   Also called "points," which are represented as a percentage of a loan amount. One point equals one percent of a loan balance. Borrowers pay discount points to reduce the interest rate for a mortgage, typically one-quarter of a percent in interest rate per each discount point paid. It is a form of prepaid interest to a lender.

Document Stamp   Evidence of a tax paid—usually made with an ink stamp. A *doc stamp,* as it is called in certain states, indicates how much tax was paid upon transfer of ownership of property. Doc-stamp tax rates can vary based upon locale. Some states don't have doc stamps, some do.

Down Payment   The amount of money initially given by the borrower to close a mortgage. The down payment equals the sales price less financing. It's the very first bit of equity you'll have in the home.

Easement   A right-of-way previously established by a third party. Easement types can vary but typically involve the right of a public utility company to cross your land to access an electrical line, for example.

Equity   The difference between the appraised value of a home and any outstanding loans recorded against the house.

Escrow   Depending upon where you live, escrow can mean two different things. On the West Coast, for example, there are escrow agents whose job it is to oversee the closing of a home loan. In other parts of the country, an escrow is a financial account set up by a lender to collect monthly installments for annual tax bills and/or hazard-insurance policy renewals.

Escrow Agent   The person or company that handles the home closing, ensuring documents are signed correctly and property transfer has legitimately changed hands.

Fannie Mae   Federal National Mortgage Association (FNMA). Originally established in 1938 by the United States government to buy Federal Housing Administration (FHA) mortgages and provide liquidity in the mortgage marketplace. In 1968, Fannie Mae's charter was changed and it now purchases conventional mortgages as well as government-insured ones. See also *Freddie Mac.*

Fed   Federal Reserve Board. Among other things, Fed board

members set overnight lending rates for banking institutions. They
don't set mortgage rates.

Fee Income   Any closing cost received by a lender or broker that is
not interest or discount points. Fee income can be in the form of
loan processing charges, underwriting fees, and the like.

FHA   Federal Housing Administration. Formed in 1934 and now a
division of the Department of Housing and Urban Development
(HUD), the FHA provides loan guarantees to lenders who make
loans under FHA guidelines.

Final Inspection   The last inspection of a property showing that a
new home being built is 100 percent complete or that a home
improvement is 100 percent complete. This inspection lets the
lender know that its collateral and loan are exactly where they
should be.

Fixed-Rate Mortgage   A mortgage whose interest rate does not
change throughout the term of the loan.

Float   Actively deciding not to "lock" or guarantee an interest rate
while a loan is being processed. A float is usually done because the
borrower believes the rates will go down.

Float Down   A mortgage loan rate that can drop as mortgage rates
drop. Usually a float down is associated with two types of float, one
being during construction of a home and the other being during
the period of an interest rate lock.

Foreclosure   The bad thing that happens when the mortgage isn't
repaid. Lenders begin the process of forcefully recovering their
collateral when borrowers fail to make loan payments. The lender
takes your house away.

Freddie Mac   Federal Home Loan Mortgage Corporation (FHLMC).
A corporation established by the United States government in 1970
to buy mortgages from lenders made under Freddie Mac
guidelines.

Fully Indexed Rate   The number reached when adding a loan's index
and the margin. This is how adjustable rates are compiled.

Funding   The actual transfer of money from a lender to a borrower.

Gift   When buying a home, the down payment and closing costs are
given to the borrower(s) instead of the funds coming from their

own accounts. Usually such gifts can only come from family members or foundations established to help new homeowners.

Ginnie Mae   Government National Mortgage Association (GNMA). A government corporation formed by the United States to guarantee loans, like VA and FHA loans, from banks and mortgage lenders.

Good Faith Estimate   A list of estimated closing costs on a particular mortgage transaction. This estimate must be provided to the loan applicants within seventy-two hours after receipt of a mortgage application by the lender or broker.

Hazard Insurance   A specific type of insurance that covers against certain destructive elements such as fire, wind, and hail. Usually it is an addition to homeowners insurance, but every home loan has a hazard rider.

HELOC   Home Equity Line of Credit. A credit line using a home as collateral. Customers write checks against the line whenever they need it and pay only on balances withdrawn. A HELOC is similar to a credit card, but secured by the property.

Homeowners Insurance   An insurance policy covering not just hazard items but also other things, such as liability or personal property.

Impound Accounts   Accounts set up by a lender to deposit the borrower's monthly portion of annual property taxes or hazard insurance. As taxes or insurance come up for renewal, the lender pays the bill using these funds. Also called *escrow accounts.*

Index   Used as the basis to establish an interest rate, usually associated with a margin. Most anything can be an index, but most common are U.S. Treasuries or similar instruments. See *fully indexed rate.*

Inspection   A structural review of the house. The goal is to look for defects in workmanship, damage to the property, or required maintenance, but an inspection does not determine the value of the property. A pest inspection looks for evidence of termites or wood ants, for example.

Intangible Tax   A state tax that collects revenue upon personal property. An intangible asset is an asset not by itself but by what it represents. A trademark is an intangible asset. It's not the trademark itself that has the value, but what it represents in terms of income.

Interest Rate   The amount charged to borrow money over a specified period of time.

Jumbo Loan   A mortgage that exceeds current conforming loan limits.

Junior Lien   A second mortgage or one that subordinates to another loan. It is not as common of a term as it used to be, and you are likely to hear it simply referred to as a "second" mortgage or "piggy back."

Land Contract   An arrangement where the buyer makes monthly payments to the seller but the ownership of the property does not change hands until the loan is paid in full. Similar to how an automobile loan works: When you pay off the car, you get the title.

Land to Value   An appraisal term that calculates the value of the land as a percentage of the total value of the home. If the land exceeds the value of the home, it's more difficult to find financing without good comparable-sales appraisal. Also called "lot to value."

Lender Policy   Title insurance that protects a mortgage from defects or previous claims of ownership.

Liability   An obligation or bill on the part of the borrower. Liabilities can be those that show up on a credit report, such as student loans or a car payment, but can also be anything else that one is obligated to pay. Liabilities on the credit report are used to determine debt ratios.

Loan   Money granted to one party with the expectation of it being repaid.

Loan Officer   The person typically responsible for helping mortgage applicants get qualified and for assisting in loan selection and loan application. Loan officers can work at banks and credit unions, and for mortgage brokerage houses or mortgage bankers.

Loan Processor   The person who gathers the required documentation for a loan application. Along with your loan officer, you'll work with this person quite a bit during your mortgage process.

Lock   The act of guaranteeing an interest rate over a predetermined period of time. Loan locks are not loan approvals; they're simply the rate your lender has agreed to give you at loan closing.

Margin A number, expressed as a percentage, that is added to a mortgage's index to determine the rate the borrower pays on the note. An index can be a six-month CD at 4 percent and the margin can be 2 percent. The interest rate the borrower pays is 4 + 2, or 6 percent. A fully indexed rate is the index plus the margin.

Market Value In an open market, the value of a property as measured by the highest price the borrower is willing to pay and the lowest price seller is willing to accept at the time of contract. Property appraisals help justify market value by comparing similar home sales in the subject property's neighborhood.

Mortgage A loan with the property being pledged as collateral. The mortgage is retired when the loan is paid in full.

Mortgage-Backed Securities Investment securities issued by Wall Street firms that are guaranteed, or collateralized, with home mortgages taken out by consumers. These securities can then be bought and sold on Wall Street.

Mortgagee The person or business making the loan.

Mortgagor The person(s) getting the loan; the borrower.

Mortgage Insurance (MI) An insurance policy that is typically required on all mortgage loans with less than 20 percent down. MI is paid by the borrower with benefits paid to the lender in order to cover the difference between the borrower's down payment and 20 percent of the sales price. If the borrower defaults on the mortgage, this difference is paid to the lender. Also called "private mortgage insurance" (PMI).

Multiple Listing Service (MLS) A central repository where real estate brokers and agents show homes and search for homes that are for sale.

Nonconforming Mortgage loan amounts above current Fannie Mae or Freddie Mac limits. Also called "jumbo" mortgages.

Note A promise to repay. A note may or may not have property involved, and may or may not be a mortgage.

NOV Notice of Value; the VA name for your appraisal.

Negative Amortization An adjustable-rate mortgage that can have two interest rates: the contract rate or the fully indexed rate. The contract rate is the minimum agreed-upon rate the consumer may pay; sometimes the contract rate is lower than the fully indexed rate. The borrower has a choice of which rate to pay, but if the contract rate is lower than the fully indexed rate, that difference is added back to the loan. If your contract payment is only $500 but the fully indexed payment is $700 and you pay only the contract rate, $200 is added back into your original loan amount. A *neg am mortgage,* as it is sometimes called for short, is not for the faint of heart, nor for those with little money down.

Origination Fee   A fee charged to cover costs associated with finding, documenting, and preparing a mortgage application; usually expressed as a percentage of the loan amount.

Owner's Policy   Title insurance made for the benefit of the homeowner.

PITI   Principal, Interest, Taxes, and Insurance. These figures are used to help determine front debt ratios. See also *debt ratio.*

PMI   Private Mortgage Insurance. See *mortgage insurance* (MI).

Points   See *discount points.*

Prepaid Interest   Daily interest collected from the day of loan closing to the first of the following month. Also can be in the form of a discount point.

Prepayment Penalty   A monetary penalty paid to the lender if the loan is paid off before its maturity or if extra payments are made on the loan. Sometimes defined as "hard" or "soft." A *hard penalty* is an automatic penalty if the loan is paid off early or extra payments are made at any time or for any amount whatsoever. A *soft penalty* only lasts for a couple of years and may allow extra payments on the loan if they do not to exceed a certain amount.

Principal   The outstanding amount owed on a loan, not including any interest due.

Realtor   A member of the National Association of Realtors (NAR). This is a registered trademark, and not all real estate agents are members of NAR.

Refinance   Obtaining a new mortgage to replace an existing one.

Sales Contract   Your written agreement, signed by both the seller and buyer, to buy or sell a home.

Second Mortgage   A mortgage that assumes a subordinate position behind a first mortgage. Sometimes called a *piggyback mortgage*. If the home goes into foreclosure, the first mortgage would be settled before the second could lay claim.

Secondary Market   A financial arena where mortgages are bought and sold, either individually or grouped together into securities backed by those mortgages. Fannie Mae and Freddie Mac are the backbone for the conventional secondary market. Other secondary markets exist for nonconforming loans, subprime loans, and others.

Seller   The person transferring ownership and all rights for your home in exchange for cash or trade.

Settlement Statement   A document showing all financial entries during the home sale, including sales price, closing costs, loan amounts, and property taxes. Your initial good faith estimate will be your first glimpse of your settlement statement. This statement, which is also called the Final HUD 1 because it is one of the final documents put together before you go to closing, is prepared by your attorney or settlement agent.

Survey   A map that shows the physical location of the structure and where it sits on the property. It also designates any easements that run across or through the property.

Title   Ownership in a property.

Title Exam   The process whereby public records are reviewed to research any previous liens on the property. Also called a "title search."

Title Insurance   An insurance policy that protects the lender, the seller, and/or the borrower against any defects or previous claims to the property being transferred or sold.

Underwriter   The person who physically approves the loan, making sure the loan meets lending guidelines, and signs off on documentation submitted.

Verification of Deposit   A written form sent by the lender to a financial institution to verify funds in an account. Also called a "VOD," this form shows how long the account has been open, everyone who has a claim to the account, and any deposits and withdrawals from or to the account.

Verification of Employment   A written form sent by the lender to an employer to verify the employment of an applicant. Also called a "VOE," this form shows how long the applicant has worked at a job, how much the person earns in salary, and any recent raises or bonuses.

Yield Spread Premium (YSP)   The difference in basis points from one rate to another offered by a wholesale lender as a result of a higher rate. The opposite of discount points that are paid to get a lower rate, YSPs are paid by the lender to get a higher rate. They are often used to offset borrower closing costs and to provide a no-point, no-fee mortgage loan.

Index